THE U.S. CAMEL CORPS
An Army Experiment

Odie B. Faulk

New York
OXFORD UNIVERSITY PRESS
1976

For LAURA, RICHARD, and NANCY

Because they have given me so much

PREFACE

Between 1848, when the Southwest became American, and 1869, when the first transcontinental railroad was completed, Westerners suffered from what has been called "the tyranny of distance." Almost 2000 miles separated the people settled along the Pacific Coast from their fellow countrymen in the Mississippi Valley—2000 miles of arid and semi-arid geography rendered doubly difficult because no major rivers flowed across it from east to west. Therefore steamboat transportation was denied them as it had not been denied in the East. The only way they or their mail could cross this region was by a journey of twenty-five days by stagecoach, a form of travel that demanded a constitution of iron and a stomach of similar strength. Otherwise both travelers and letters had to make a tedious six-month voyage by sea around South America or a three-month split trip by ship by way of Panama.

Because of the hardships few Americans crossed the continent more than once. Those pilgrims wanting to move to California did so and then tended to stay there. Only when gold or silver was discovered in the desert country did people move to the region in large numbers; for quick wealth they would endure almost any hardship. Only when railroad tracks were laid in this region did settlements grow.

During the twenty-one years from acquisition to completion of the first transcontinental railroad, soldiers of the United States Army were the only residents of much of the West. Their task was to protect the transient pilgrims from their own ignorance and from the Indians. Supplying these soldiers by traditional means—wagons drawn by mules and oxen or by packmules— proved difficult and expensive; always there were those thinking of good alternatives. One of these was the introduction of camels, first proposed in 1836 by a soldier and adopted by Congress in 1855 as an experiment at the urging of Secretary of War Jefferson Davis.

Camels were brought to the United States in 1856, according to the directive of Congress, to test their fitness "for military purposes." In the years immediately following, the animals showed their capacities, earning grudging respect from the officers who directed their efforts. Yet the camel was never adopted as a Western animal, not because of any limitations on his part but because he was alien, because there was opposition from local settlers and officers bound by tradition, and because other animals in the West reacted strongly to his presence. Before he could receive a fair test, the Civil War intervened, ending the experiment, and after the war the railroad was built west at a rapid clip. Today only the legend of a few wild camels and a few obscure monuments remain of this experiment.

The attempt to introduce camels shows that some officers in the Army were willing to adapt rapidly to geographic necessity, just as it shows that other officers were hidebound traditionalists. These animals contributed to opening the West by carrying supplies on expeditions that surveyed a wagon road along the 35th parallel and another survey into the Big Bend country. And they performed some of the dirtiest work in the West when they were used to transport salt and ore to and from mines in Nevada and

Arizona. They were exotic pioneers who had too short a time to demonstrate their capabilities.

In writing this book, I have been incurred many debts. Dr. Charles Dollar of the National Archives aided me in securing copies of all the documents in the Camel File of the Old Army and Navy Records Branch, for which I am deeply grateful. Other aspects of the story I researched at the Arizona Historical Society in Tucson when I worked there; the files of that institution constitute a rich vein for a historian to work. The staff of the Library at Oklahoma State University, as always, proved most helpful, as did those working at other institutions I visited. I also thank Patty McCrabb, who typed parts of the manuscript, and Dr. Carl N. Tyson, who listened and made suggestions.

In the past I have dedicated several books to my wife, Laura, who encourages and helps me through the process of drafting a manuscript, who proofreads, and who acts as a critic in the finest sense of the word. Other books I have dedicated to my children, Richard and Nancy, for the interest and preference they have stated for one or another topic. To these three this book is dedicated as my way of saying, "Thank you."

Stillwater, Oklahoma   O. B. F.
Summer 1975

CONTENTS

1
INTRO-
DUCTION

Most Americans suddenly discovered the Great West between 1844 and 1850. True, there had been a few thousand hardy pioneers trekking across the Oregon Trail to the Pacific Northwest and a few hundred to California prior to 1844, just as there had been Mountain Men seeking a fortune from beaver pelts taken in icy streams in the Rockies and foolhardy Texans trying to operate a republic in a former Mexican state. And there had been civilian and Army explorers moving through the area for four decades, their reports and reminiscences published for public reading. Yet to most Americans the country to the west of Iowa and Louisiana was as unknown as the Ukraine or Mongolia.

Then came the election of 1844 in which James K. Polk, the Democratic nominee for President, spoke of expanding the United States by annexing Texas and by achieving a settlement with England about the ownership of Oregon. Whig candidate Henry Clay, the Kentucky hotspur, opposed—or tried to avoid—both of these issues. When Polk won the election, events moved rapidly thereafter. Congress, on February 28, 1845, enacted a joint resolution authorizing Texas to enter the Union, and Polk proclaimed it the twenty-eighth state on December 29 that same year. In June the following year the British proposed an extension of the 49th parallel westward to the Pacific as the boundary between Canada and the United States, and the Senate immediately ratified a treaty to that effect.

During the war with Mexico, which began in May of 1846, the Army of the West made its epic march to California under the leadership of General Stephen Watts Kearny, while a battalion of Mormons, led by Colonel Philip St. George Cooke, opened a wagon road from Santa Fe to San Diego. By January of 1847 the country from New Mexico to California had been added to the Union by force, although the United States agreed in the Treaty of Guadalupe Hidalgo, signed on February 2, 1848, to pay Mexico $15,000,000 for this "cession." Simultaneously Brigham Young was leading the members of the Church of Jesus Christ of Latter-Day Saints into the Great Basin to settle beside the Great Salt Lake. The nation was flooded with published memoirs, official documents, and histories. Awareness of the West grew.

Simultaneously came electrifying news: gold had been discovered in California. The few thousands who hurried west in 1848 were but the vanguard of tens and hundreds of thousands to make the trip the following year and become immortalized as "Forty-Niners." By 1850 the western population had grown so large that California was granted statehood, while New Mexico and Utah became territories (as had Oregon in 1848). In short, the pioneers who had settled the United States in such an orderly progression from the Atlantic Seaboard west to Iowa, Missouri, and Texas suddenly moved halfway across the continent to populate the West Coast and selected areas along the way.

Between these areas of settlement, American frontiersmen found a great amount of land, most of it totally unfamiliar to them. Immediately west of the timberline running from Texas northward to the region west of the Great Lakes (the line where the amount of rainfall annually dropped below twenty inches), the westering pilgrim found what was called "broken country," a region that was gradually flattening to become the Great Plains. This was a land formed by the silt carried out of the Rocky Mountains by a multitude of rivulets, creeks, and rivers: the Missouri, the Platte, the Arkansas, the Cimarron, the Canadian, the Red, the Trinity, and the Brazos. This was a region subject to winds that seemed eternal, winds that blew year-round to freeze in winter, parch in summer, and brought seasonal rains that turned all into a vast marsh. In this area which, in the language of modern meteorologists, has a continental weather pattern—meaning it gets all extremes of weather known on the North American continent—the storms of spring bring tornados, hail, and rains, while the "northers" of winter bring sleet and blinding snowstorms; and in the summer these same winds blow from the south up into the mountains to melt the snow and bring rivers rushing down silt-laden to form yet another layer on the plains.

The feature the frontiersmen first noticed about this plains country was the absence of trees. The United States of the Atlantic Seaboard, the Gulf Coast Region, and the Mississippi Valley was timbered, well watered, and fertile. In climate and resources it was little different from Western Europe, except that it was still unexploited when the colonists first arrived. Nothing in that region had prepared the frontier descendants of those colonists for the treeless plains of the trans-Mississippi region; to them the area seemed too open and made them feel uncomfortably defenseless, for there was no place to hide.

Next the pioneers noticed the grass. The type of vegetation most associated with the region was usually called "shortgrass," for the subsoil did not hold enough moisture to allow the extensive root systems needed by taller grasses. The more level the ground, the more the grass dominated. However, where the land was more broken, other kinds of plants grew: gnarled mesquite trees, some thorny shrubs, and cactus. They mingled with the blue gramma or buffalo grass which was the home of wild hogs, white-tailed deer, wild turkeys, prairie dogs, pronghorn antelope, ground squirrels, and millions of field mice and jack rabbits. Also, there were a thousand varieties of birds which added a dash of color, a warble of song, and a sudden thrashing of wings. They combined with the other noises and colors of the region to form something unique in the American experience.

The best-known native animal to feed on the shortgrass on the plains was the American bison, or buffalo. No predatory animal in this vast region from Canada to Texas was capable of killing these great shaggy beasts. If they wandered into the foothills of the Rocky Mountains, grizzly bears and wolves occasionally would try to feed on them but usually even these animals would tackle only a solitary buffalo, preferably one that was young or old or wounded—somehow feeble. A buffalo bull made a formidable enemy, for he often weighed a ton, and with his horns and hooves he could fight off most any attacker. Moreover, buffalo were difficult to surprise, for when the herd fed an old cow usually stood guard; she was quick to see moving objects, for these animals had extremely good eyesight. Moreover, buffalo were good runners; once a herd stampeded, only a good horse could keep up with it. And buffalo were equally good swimmers, crossing broad rivers to reach new feeding grounds.

On the plains of the Midwest, the buffalo spent their lives, grazing contentedly, wallowing in sand to clean themselves, drinking from creeks and streams, and increasing their numbers. Calves weighed from twenty-five to forty pounds at birth. They were orange-red in color until about three months of age; then they assumed the dark color of the adults, blackish or yellowish brown. By the fall after their birth, calves weighed some 400 pounds and had begun to grow the long, thick coat of wool that would protect them from the wintery cold. When American pioneers first reached the plains, there were an estimated 5,000,000 to 8,000,000 buffalo in the southern herd and an equal number to the north.

By this same time, however, wild horses were contesting with the buffalo for pasturage. Introduced by Spaniards, a few of these animals had escaped to run wild and to increase until they had spread all across the American West and numbered some 10,000,000.

The pioneer who ventured out onto the plains also noticed that the rainfall diminished the farther west he went. Just beyond the timberline the annual rainfall averaged nearly twenty inches, but it dropped off rapidly as he moved toward the setting sun. And when at last he came to the place where less than ten inches fell each year, he had arrived in the desert country. However, by this time the frontiersman generally was not looking down at the land; rather he was looking up—at the mightiest range of mountains to be seen on the North American continent.

Mountains differ from humans in their growth cycle. In fact, they are exact opposites. They are born tall and grow shorter with age; they are born bald on their tops and, as they wash down to the size of hills, trees gradually cover their summits. They are born with wrinkles that slowly fill with sediment as rain and wind do their work. Like humans, however, mountains are born with a cry of anguish as they are thrust into life by a geologic upheaval; yet their death is as quiet as the falling rains and whispering winds that reduce them first to hills and, at last, to broad plains.

In the West there are two major ranges of mountains: the Rockies, a jutting chain that extends southward from Alaska through Canada and down from Idaho-Montana to New Mexico, then south into Mexico—and ultimately to the tip of South America; and the Coastal Range, also known as the Sierra Nevada, which begins in British Columbia and runs down the West Coast almost adjacent to the Pacific Ocean. Moving from the plains into these mountains, a traveler quickly noted a rapid change in climate and vegetation. At the base of the mountains there is usually water in the form of small running streams. The moisture that evaporates from it mingles with the cool air blown down from the heights above, and the winds that swirl downward through the gaps and passes allows this moisture to serve as a means of natural air conditioning.

At the base of these mountains the pines begin. In the Southwestern United States this is the piñon pine (also spelled pinyon). Twisted and gnarled by its semi-desert, semi-mountain environment, the piñon is capable of reaching fifty feet in height, but usually is much smaller. The Indians and the Spaniards who

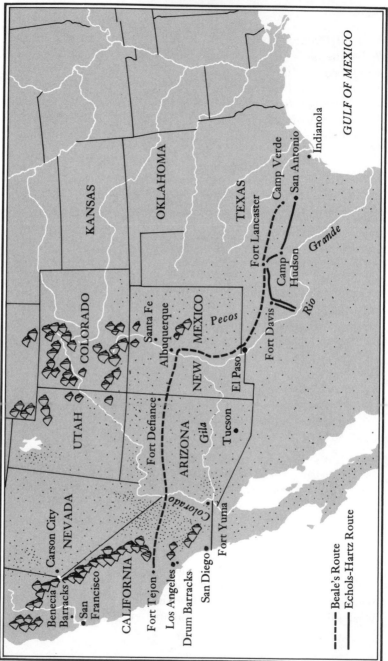

GULF OF MEXICO

Indianola

San Antonio

Camp Verde

Rio Grande

Fort Lancaster

Camp Hudson

TEXAS

Fort Davis

El Paso

Pecos

Santa Fe

Albuquerque

NEW MEXICO

COLORADO

KANSAS

OKLAHOMA

Tucson

Gila

ARIZONA

Fort Defiance

UTAH

Colorado

Fort Yuma

San Diego

Drum Barracks

Los Angeles

Fort Tejon

CALIFORNIA

NEVADA

Carson City

Benecia Barracks

San Francisco

- - - - Beale's Route

———— Echols-Hartz Route

settled there before the arrival of Americans used the piñon for timber for their homes, as firewood for their stoves, and as food in the form of the edible nuts which grow between the scales of their cones. If there is any odor most associated with the Southwest from the earliest times to the present, especially in rural areas, it is the pungent smell of piñon logs burning in cookstoves and fireplaces.

At the base of northern mountains—and above the 6000-foot level in the Southwest—is the ponderosa pine mingled with occasional stands of aspen. Under these trees live a profusion of small animals: big gray rock squirrels, which make their nests in rocky crevices on the ground; skunks, chipmunks, ground squirrels, foxes, weasels, rats, mice, even mule deer. The red-faced warbler, pygmy nuthatches, and broad-tailed hummingbirds scurry after insects, while tassel-eared squirrels hurry out of the way of deer and fuss at them for disturbing their hunt for food.

Two to three thousand feet higher in the mountains, the ponderosa pine begins to thin out, replaced by Douglas fir mingled with quiet groves of aspen. Mule deer are more numerous, and blue grouse come out early in the morning and late in the evening to hunt for seeds and berries. The enemy of all big animals at this elevation is the mountain lion (also known as a panther, puma, and cougar). Black bears wander the region with few quarrels, but run from their larger cousin, the grizzly, a brute of great strength and short temper. Only rarely seen are big-horn sheep, although some do come this far down the mountains on occasion.

Still higher up the mountains the Douglas fir thin out to be replaced by Foxtail pine and Englemann spruce. At this height the vegetation is similar to that found on ground-level in Labrador; these are subarctic trees, yet at this elevation, even in Arizona and New Mexico, the traveler is in a subarctic zone. And a few animals can be found, principally porcupines; they gnaw the bark off the trees to eat the layer just underneath. Big-horn sheep inhabit this level during the winter months.

The few travelers who go on up the mountains at last come above the tree line to a height where nothing but a few grasses, sedges, and herbs grow. No trees are able to withstand the extreme cold and the gale-blast winds. This is an area known as alpine tundra, and on it can be found in summer surprisingly beautiful flowers, a few hardy rodents living among the rocks, and big-horn sheep.

These ranges of mountains, the Rockies and the Sierra, cause the deserts between them. The prevailing wind direction in this latitude is west to east; moisture-laden clouds blowing inland from the Pacific Ocean are forced to rise when they come to the Coastal Sierra, and in the process they dump their rains on the western slope of these mountains. To the east the Rockies serve as a barrier to the moisture-laden air sucked north from the Gulf of Mexico by the winds of spring, and this rain falls on the eastern slope of these mountains. Thus between the two chains of mountains the air is dry most of the year, and less than ten inches of rain falls on the land—which therefore is desert.

The deserts of the West are of two types: low and high. However, most Americans of the nineteenth century, like their twentieth-century descendants, think only of the region in southern Arizona and New Mexico when they hear the word "desert." The plant most associated with this low desert is the saguaro cactus. This is fitting, for the saguaro indeed is the king of cacti. Growing occasionally to fifty feet and more in height and ten tons in weight, it throws out branches that gracefully curve until it has the appearance of a candelabrum. Yet the part visible to the eye is less than half the plant; it sends down a shallow network of roots radiating thirty-five feet in all directions.

In the shadow of these desert giants is a rich variety of other plants, shrubs, and trees. Sagebrush, saltbush, cholla, palo verde, ocotillo, mesquite—much of it prickly with thorns and spines and all with deep root systems—hold a strong footing. These do not grow close to one another, for water is too scarce; each must fight for survival in its own wide plot of ground. Thus the first plant to establish a root network squeezes out all newcomers. A few scant clumps of hardy grass spring up between these plants to absorb the spring rains, but during the dry period these wither away. The rest flower, grow, and produce seeds in the spring, then go almost dormant during the dry period, and most have a tough, thick, outer skin to hold in moisture absorbed during the wet part of the year. This short growing period accounts for the slow maturity of desert plants; a saguaro cactus, for example, will be only about four inches tall at age ten, requiring a hundred years or more to reach maturity.

Animal life is equally abundant in this area. On a single saguaro can be found weevil larvae, rats and mice, moths and other insects, cactus wrens and a variety of their cousins: the organ-pipe, staghorn, hedgehog, pincushion, rainbow, and claret-cup wrens. And Gila woodpeckers gouge holes in the sides of these desert giants to lay their eggs and raise their young. Other forms of desert life include the rock squirrel, which lives on the ground and resembles the ground squirrel of other regions; snakes of a dozen and more varieties, most of them poisonous; jack rabbits; lizards, among which is the famed Gila monster; birds, most notorious of which is the road runner; spiders, including the tarantula and the black widow; and mammals that include the skunk, the coyote, the badger, the raccoon, the deer, the bobcat, and the peccary (also known as the javelina and the wild hog). Most of these animals, unless they are night foragers, come out only in the early morning or late afternoon; at midday and early afternoon the temperature often rises above 130° and can kill anything that stays out too long.

To the west of this Southwestern desert, past the Colorado River, is the Imperial Valley, and a hundred miles north of it is Death Valley. Yet this most savage and inhospitable area is rarely a barren waste of rolling sand dunes. Even in Death Valley there are a dozen species of lizards, more than thirty types of mammals, well over 600 species of plants, and, where there is water, even fish.

North of this low desert country is the high desert of northern New Mexico and Arizona and southern Utah and Nevada, a land of little grass, a few hardy shrubs, and almost no trees, which is part of the drainage basin of the Colorado River. This is a region of sandstone buttes carved by wind and rain to stand as sentinels over a land seemingly dead, a land similar in many respects to the desert north of it known as the Great (or Intermountain) Basin.

This occupies almost all of Nevada, much of western Utah, and part of Oregon, Wyoming, and California. The low point of this region is the Great Salt Lake, a body of water more briny than the ocean; the moisture trapped there has no outlet other than evaporation. Other shallow lakes form during the occasional rains, but they soon evaporate into salt flats; extinct lakes there include Bonneville Salt Flats and Lahontan. This vast plateau contains little vegetation except near its edges where desert shrubs cling hardily to life; no trees are to be found in this region.

Because most Americans crossing this region rarely tried to climb the mountains—and thus did not see the profusion of plants and animals there—they wrote of the West as a desert, just as had the first explorers of the region. Lieutenant Zebulon M. Pike, who explored into Colorado, New Mexico, and Texas in 1806–1807, and Major Stephen H. Long, who searched for the headwaters of the Arkansas River in 1820, wrote that the Great Plains constituted a "Great American Desert" on which no one except Indians could live; Long stated, "in regard to this extensive section of country between the Missouri River and the Rocky Mountains we do not hesitate in giving the opinion that it is almost wholly unfit for cultivation and of course uninhabitable by a people depending upon agriculture for their subsistence." [1] He concluded that although some of the soil was fertile and that some timber and water existed in isolated spots, the area could never be of any practical value except to a nomadic people. And neither Pike nor Long saw the real desert.

However, by 1850 this vast region was being crossed by thousands of people annually as they tried to reach Oregon or California or Utah or New Mexico. These pilgrims had no rivers over which to travel rapidly, as had pioneers in the eastern part of the United States. Flowing into the Mississippi were several rivers that had their origins in the Rockies, but they were capable of bearing steamers only a short distance onto the Great Plains; soon they became too shallow to be of any use. Between the mountain ranges was only one river of any size, the Colorado, but it flowed from north to south for the length of Arizona's western border and then turned eastward through the Grand Canyon into the rugged mountains of western Colorado; thus it was of no value as a carrier of people, mail, and goods.

Those people seeking to cross this region found, therefore, that their options were few: they could board a ship for the six-month-long voyage around Cape Horn; they could board a ship, sail to Panama, cross the Isthmus, and board another vessel to sail to California or Oregon; or they could make the long trek overland by one of the three major trails. The southernmost of these, the Gila Trail, began in Texas, followed an Army road to El Paso, and then led to California across the route blazed by the Mormon Battalion during the Mexican War: to Las Cruces and Tucson, north along the banks of the Santa Cruz to the Gila, down the Gila to Yuma Crossing, and finally to San Diego. Or the pilgrim might begin at St. Louis or Independence, Missouri, go west along the Platte River to South Pass, move by various routes across the Great Basin, then labor through passes in the Sierra to the Pacific slope. Finally, there was the Oregon Trail; this began, as did the central (or Humboldt) trail, in the St. Louis and Independence area, and followed the Platte to South Pass; there the pioneer bound for Oregon crossed the Rockies to the Snake River, went down it to the Columbia River, and followed that stream into Oregon.

On all three of these overland routes the principal means of travel was the wagon. Most frontier Americans owned one (and oxen and tools); they loaded it with food, their furniture, and family treasures and set out in the spring when the grass along the trail was high enough to sustain their stock. Once on the prairie they were frightened by the spring storms that produced lightning such as they had never seen, along with hail and rain. Then they climbed steadily until they reached South Pass or crossed the continental divide in western New Mexico to drop down into the desert. Those who had thought that nothing was so deadly as plodding through the choking dust of the desert forgot that annoyance when they encountered the hardships of passing wagons and oxen over the Sierra and then lowering them by rope down precipitous canyons. In the words of one Westerner, these pilgrims set out on this 2000-mile trek armed with "the courage of ignorance." Lieutenant Cave J. Couts, protecting boundary surveyors at Yuma Crossing in 1849, wrote of the gold-seekers swarming toward California, "They . . . are willing to keep me talking and making way-Bills [maps] for them from sun-up until sun-down and from sun-down to sun-up. In addition to this they beg me for rations day in and day out." Apparently many of these Forty-Niners were extremely hungry, for Couts stated, "From the way they shovel down the pork and bread, is sufficient proof of its rarity, and sugar and coffee! Some are worse than ratholes to fill." [2]

Three animals were used by Americans trekking westward during this period: horses, oxen, and mules. Most of the horses used to pull wagons were simply farm animals—definitely not thoroughbred Percherons, Clydesdales, or Belgians. These were sturdy, dependable, and hard-working, but only so long as they received a steady supplement of grain in their diet. They could not subsist on prairie grass and desert plants alone. Riding horses likewise tended to be of mixed breed, and they also needed a morning feeding with grain. Only the Southwestern mustang (or quarter-horse) was capable of subsisting on what it found to eat along the way. This horse was descended from stock brought from Spain to the New World. In the Southwest some of these animals strayed, multiplied, and formed wild herds that eventually ranged the Great Plains and into the Rockies. Of scrubby appearance and slight stature, they were wiry, fleet, and untamed. However, those riding these animals found they had to have several remounts, for the Spanish mustang did not get enough strength from the grass he consumed to allow him to carry rider and saddle all day.

Oxen proved far more dependable as draft animals than horses did. These sturdy animals, descendants of the oxen of Biblical days, suffered far fewer diseases than horses, were far gentler, less expensive to feed, and almost impossible to stampede. A good pair of oxen cost about fifty dollars, slightly less than one good horse. Moreover, an ox had one other advantage: if disabled he could be slaughtered and his meat added to the daily menu. Even then, few Americans could bring themselves to eat horse flesh except as a last resort.

Most expensive of the three was the mule. A healthy mule cost from $100 to $150, and experienced frontiersmen gladly paid this sum, just as they ignored the laughter of greenhorns at the lack of nobility about such mounts. The preferred hybrid was the Spanish mule, not his American counterpart from the East. The Spanish mule, specially bred over several centuries for service in arid and semiarid country, was small in stature, rarely weighing more than seven or eight hundred pounds. Ranging in color from yellowish- and grayish-white to coal black, the Spanish mule was barrel-chested and small hoofed, and, argued Americans who knew both breeds well, they were higher in intelligence than their Eastern-bred cousins. They had great strength and endurance, could work with poorer food and less water than horses, and recovered more quickly after long periods of hard work. In addition, their flinty hooves withstood the rigors of prairie grass better than those of oxen, and they withstood the shocks and abrasions of rocks and granite outcroppings in the mountains. Josiah Gregg, a Santa Fe trader, noted of the mule, "This animal is in fact to the Mexican what the camel has always been to the Arab—invaluable for the transportation of freight over sandy deserts and mountainous roads, where no other means of conveyance could be used to such advantage." [3] A comment sent east to the Fort Smith *Gazette* by a Forty-Niner showed the esteem in which the experienced pioneer held the mule: ". . . To anyone starting from Ft. Smith for California, I would say get two good mules . . . one for riding and another for packing . . . and he will arrive in better order than when he started. Some horses in our company failed entirely; others have barely got through. . . . Mules have fattened from the start." [4]

Livestock was a prime target of the native tribes living on the Great Plains, in the mountains, and on the deserts of the West, who were angered at the thousands of pioneers crossing their land. Many times they attacked wagon trains to kill and steal. To protect Americans from the Indians—and from their own ignorance—soldiers were sent into the West to found forts and ride on patrol. Each of them had to be supplied with feed, grain for their horses, and ammunition for their weapons. The farther one of the posts was from supply by water, the more expensive the freighting proved. For example, in 1849 when soldiers were sent to establish Fort Yuma, astride the Gila Trail, quartermaster officers contracted with teamsters to bring supplies the 180 miles from San Diego overland to the new post. Captain Rufus Ingalls, the quartermaster at Fort Yuma, later said, "From San Diego to Fort Yuma there is but one practable [sic] wagon route, and it passes over, perhaps, the worst and most irksome desert for beasts in the world. There are more extensive deserts than this great 'American desert'; but considering the distance to be passed over, it is as hazardous and pernicious as so much of Sahara or Gobi." He also noted that in 1851 Fort Yuma had to be abandoned for a time because of "the enormous expense of furnishing supplies and the small amount furnished." The cost was $500 to $800 per ton—for moving goods only 180 miles.[5]

In addition, the settlers of California and Oregon were demanding some fast way to communicate with the East other than the slow method of sending letters by sea. In 1848 the Post Office Department had awarded contracts for a semi-monthly service by sea between New York and San Francisco; under the terms of this agreement the United States Steamship Company carried the mail to Panama, it then traveled overland to Panama City, and finally it went to California on ships owned by the Pacific Mail Steamship Company. This trip was supposed to be made in thirty days, but usually it took much longer.

Little wonder, therefore, that many thoughtful Americans were seeking some fast, reasonable means of moving people, mail, and goods across to the West. By the early 1850s steam transportation—the railroad—seemed to offer the best solution to the national need. Already many hundreds of miles of track had been laid in the East, showing that railroads could provide dependable, fast, and inexpensive transportation. Technical experts, when queried, stated that a transcontinental railroad could be built across the United States and that it would take just ten days for a train to run from the East Coast to the West Coast.

An early proponent of a transcontinental railroad was Asa Whitney, a merchant from New York City who was engaged in the China trade by sea. In 1845 Whitney went before Congress to describe his plan to lay track from some site on the Great Lakes, already linked to the East Coast by canal and rails, to some port on the coast of Oregon (California yet belonged to Mexico in 1845). Whitney argued that Congress should aid the project by giving the builders a swath of land sixty miles wide as an inducement. However, a majority of congressmen felt the scheme was impractical, visionary, and too expensive ever to show a profit.

Next to take up this cry was James Gadsden of South Carolina. At a railroaders' convention in Memphis that same year of 1845, he argued that track should be laid from some point in the South across to the Pacific. Sam Houston, aging hero of the Texas Revolution and a United States senator after Texas entered the Union, advocated the same thing; they urged that a line should run from Galveston, Texas, to San Diego. Such a route, said Houston, would not be too costly because of the short distance involved, yet would allow quick transport of goods, mail, and passengers by sea from Galveston to the East Coast. Northerners replied that track logically should run from Chicago to Puget Sound or Portland.

By 1852 few people doubted that a railroad could be built. The questions yet to be answered were the route—northern or southern—and the method of finance. While sectional interests seemed to dictate the route advocated by each "expert," all agreed that federal funds would have to be appropriated to aid the project. A transcontinental line, like other railroads, would make its money by carrying people, freight, and mail, yet this one would cross vast stretches of territory virtually empty of people. Because the transcontinental would serve the national interest rather than make a profit, ran the usual argument, it would have to receive some type of federal funding, either in the form of a loan or as a guaranteed subsidy. And after the line was open, it probably would operate at a loss, and thus a continual subsidy would have to be given. Proponents of the projected line, northern and southern, realized that the federal treasury was not rich enough to pay for the building and operating of more than one transcontinental, just as they knew there would not be enough business even for one line to operate at a profit. Thus the argument raged even more bitterly about the *best* route over which the one road should run.

Out of this argument between Southerners and Northerners came a call for accurate information about the various possible routes. Therefore in 1853 Congress appropriated $150,000 for the Army to find the most practicable and economical route for a railroad from the Mississippi River to the Pacific Ocean. Apparently congressmen hoped that only one good route would be found, thereby ending the growing sectional quarrel about where track should be laid. Assigned the task of surveying these routes was the Corps of Topographical Engineers, the map-making branch of the Army. The reports returned to Congress showed that there was not *one* good route, but rather four of them, each with its individual merits and demerits: one near the Canadian border that terminated at Puget Sound, a second through the north-central part of the country to San Francisco, a third through the south-central region to Los Angeles, and a fourth along the thirty-second parallel to San Diego.[6]

These reports left Congress deadlocked by the sectional interests of North and South and Midwest—and unable to vote a subsidy (not until Southerners withdrew from Congress at the outbreak of the Civil War did Congress finally vote a federal charter to the Union Pacific and Central Pacific). Meanwhile, Californians and Oregonians were without a fast mail service, and the Army had no cheap way to supply its posts. The search for an alternate means of transport continued. Inasmuch as most of the West was commonly referred to as a "desert," the animal that next came to mind was the camel.

Apparently the first person seriously to discuss the possibility of importing camels to America for use as beasts of burden in the West was George H. Crosman. A native of Georgia and a graduate of the United States Military Academy, Crosman was appointed a brevet second lieutenant in the 3rd Infantry on July 1, 1823. Promoted to first lieutenant in 1828, he saw duty in Florida during the Seminole wars. One year before he was promoted to captain in 1837, he already was advocating to his superiors in Washington that camels should be imported and tested. His suggestions met with no action, but he continued to discuss the possibility with anyone who would listen. In 1838 he transferred to the Quartermaster Corps and was assigned to Boston as the assistant quartermaster there. In this city he held lengthy discussions with E. F. Miller of Ipswich, Massachusetts, who was the son of retired General James Miller. On April 21, 1843, Miller wrote Crosman:

> In conversation, some time since, we were discussing the practicability of adding another facility for army transportation, in the southwestern country . . . by the introduction of the camel, an animal whose services for transportation and other purposes, have always been held in the highest estimation among the nations of the east, although hitherto unused in this country.
>
> It seems to me that these creatures would furnish a most valuable aid to the transportation department if they could be introduced & successfully propagated in the southwest. . . . For strength in carrying burthens, for patient endurance of labor, and privation of food, water & rest, and in some respects for *speed* also, the camel and dromedary (as the Arabian camel is called) are unrivalled among animals. The ordinary loads for camels are from seven to nine to ten hundred pounds each, and with these they can travel from thirty to forty miles per day, for many days in succession. They will go without water, and with but little food, for six or eight days, or it is said even longer. Their feet are alike well suited for traversing grassy or sandy plains, or rough, rocky & hilly paths, and they require no shoeing. . . .
>
> Should the Department desire it, more definite information can easily be furnished as to the probable expense of importation &c.[7]

Crosman sent Miller's letter, along with his own recommendation, to General S. Jesup, quartermaster general of the Army. Jesup was not impressed, replying on May 6, ". . . I am inclined to doubt the propriety of such a measure—matters of that kind can be more safely left to enlightened private enterprise: at all events this is no time for experiments on the part of the Government—the Treasury is too poor to do more than provide for the indispensable wants of the public service." [8]

Miller's letter, along with that of Captain Crosman, gave a fair indication of the assets of the camel. Author Charles Lummis once wrote, "Man needed a straight-out servant, and so God built him the mule. And a true servant he is, from the time he begins to walk until the breath leaves his worn-out shell." [9] The Bedouins of Arabia state the camel's case more succinctly, calling the beast *"Ata Allah"*—God's Gift. Indeed, the animal seems just that.

Scientists now believe, from fossils they have uncovered, that the *camelidae* family originated on the North American continent some 40,000,000 years ago. Originally about a foot high, the animal gradually grew in size, developed into several distinct species, and spread across the earth. In South America are the vicuña, the guanaco, the llama, and the alpaca, while in the region between Siberia and central China is the Bactrian camel with two humps; the dromedary (derived from the Greek *dromos*, meaning racecourse) chose to live in the desert region of Africa and it became the most numerous—and useful—member of the family. Only in North America, original home of the animal, did no descendant survive to serve man.

Every feature of the camel seems designed for its harsh desert environment. It has extremely mobile lips that can gather food without his having to stick out his tongue (and lose moisture), and it will eat anything it can get into its mouth. Bushes with thorns, scrub desert plants, weeds so bitter that other animals avoid them—he eats all with apparent delight. Inside his mouth are thirty-four teeth: sixteen in the upper jaw, including two incisors, two canines, and twelve molars; and eighteen in the lower jaw, including six incisors, two canines, and ten molars. In the front part of its mouth the teeth are razor sharp, capable of biting through pulpy plants which neither horse nor mule can crop. A true ruminant, the animal has four stomachs, passing its food

Typical scene in Egypt of camels in use. Drawing by Gwinn Harris Heap.

from one back to the mouth for further chewing and then to the next stomach; his digestive system is designed to extract the last bit of nourishment and moisture from every scrap of food.

The camel's most remarkable feature, however, is his hump. It is composed of fatty tissue equal to one-fifth of his body weight—and is not, as commonly thought, a reservoir for water. When the camel cannot get a drink, it extracts moisture from fatty tissue throughout its body; scientific tests have shown that a camel can lose up to one-fourth of his body weight without losing his strength. When the beast has drunk his fill and has not been worked too hard, his hump is plump and firm; but when he is thirsty and has been hard worked, the fat in the hump is dehydrated and it becomes flaccid, sometimes even reducing to little more than skin. On long journeys when the animal is carrying a heavy load, the hump gradually wastes away, but rest, good food, and water will restore it to its full shape. Normally the beast will drink every three days, twenty to thirty gallons at a time, but its body is so efficient at extracting moisture from its food that camels have been known to go as long as ten months without taking in water.

As protection from blowing sand, the camel can close his ears and nostrils tightly, just as it has double eyelashes for the purpose of protecting its eyes from sand. The eyes themselves project from the head, but are inclined slightly downward so that the sight of the animal normally is directed more downward than forward; therefore the camel normally is looking where his feet are to be placed next, which in part accounts for its surefootedness.

The feet of the camel are so designed that they are equally adapted to treading on sand and on sharp rocks. Each hoof is composed of two long toes united by and resting on an elastic cushion fitted with a tough sole. Each foot is extremely wide at the bottom, but narrows rapidly to a slender shin. When his foot comes to rest on the ground, it spreads, affording it a broader base of support than any animal of comparable size. Contrary to his public image, however, the camel prefers not to walk on sand; most of the desert is a hard, compact, gravelly surface, and this the beast likes. He is most unhappy on mud, however, for there he sinks readily and cannot move easily.[10]

Domesticated for so many centuries that he no longer lives wild anywhere, the camel averages almost seven feet in height, ten feet in length, and 1000 pounds in weight. Most commonly their color ranges from fawn to brown to black, although a few are white. Especially preferred in Africa are those of a rose tint.[11] Normally desert owners of camels pack them with a load of about 500 pounds, under which burden the beast will average slightly more than two miles per hour.[12] George P. Marsh, who lectured extensively in the United States about camels in the mid-1850s, noted that the "length of the caravan day's journey, when there is no special motive for haste, is regulated by the distance between wells and pasture-grounds; but it is seldom less than ten, and more frequently twelve or fourteen hours, and in most countries the entire day's journey is performed without a halt." [13] Unloaded the camel is capable of running ten miles an hour for as many as eighteen hours.

Born after a gestation period of almost a year, a baby camel is virtually helpless for several months. At an age of four or five the young beast is broken to work; this is accomplished by inserting a nose plug to which lead reins are attached. The driver then leads the young animal by pulling on the lead reins; however, great care must be exercised, for too light a pull avails nothing, while too strong a pull will tear the animal's nostrils and turn him into a raging killer. Once the camel is trained, it will work for the rest of its life, and it has a normal life expectancy of about forty years.

Such were the reports spreading in the United States about the camel. However, the few American travelers who had seen these desert beasts by the early 1850s tended to write only about the positive qualities they possessed: how they were used to carry trade goods northward from black Africa to the Mediterranean and back again, that they carried armies across the desert, even that the Persian army in the 1830s was using camels as platforms for small, mobile artillery—"gunships of the desert." Few travelers reported the liabilities and limitations of the camel or wrote of its temperament. These features would become known only after the federal government committed itself to an experiment with them involving the United States Army.

2
THE
CAMEL
APPROPRIATION

George H. Crosman continued to write and speak about the desirability of bringing camels to the United States to be used in the Southwest, but he received little encouragement at the official level. As a captain of Quartermaster, he marched into Texas with General Zachary Taylor's command, and for his "gallant and meritorious conduct" at the Battle of Palo Alto, he was breveted a major on May 8, 1846. Less than a year later, on March 3, 1847, he was promoted to the rank of major in the Quartermaster Corps, and after the war he was assigned to duty in Washington, D.C.[1]

In that city he met another Quartermaster officer and fellow major, Henry C. Wayne. Born in Savannah, Georgia, in 1815, Wayne was a graduate of the Military Academy at the late age of twenty-three, and was appointed a second lieutenant of artillery. Promoted to first lieutenant in 1842, he transferred to the Quartermaster Corps just after the outbreak of the Mexican War with the rank of captain. For his "gallant and meritorious conduct" at the battles of Contreras and Churubusco, during the campaign led by General Winfield Scott to conquer Mexico City, Wayne was breveted a major; afterward he, like Crosman, was stationed in Washington, D.C.[2] He would serve there for seven years.

Wayne became a ready convert to the concept of using camels in the American West, and with the enthusiasm of the convert he set about "educating" members of Congress and the secretary of war. His efforts, like those of Crosman, brought little more result than laughter—with one major exception: Jefferson Davis, a senator from Mississippi and chairman of the committee on military affairs, became, like Wayne, a convert, but he eventually would rise to a position of such influence that he could make the dream a reality.

There was little in Davis' background to explain why he so enthusiastically adopted the dream of importing camels. Davis was born to middle-class parents on June 3, 1808, in Todd County, Kentucky, but the family soon moved to Mississippi to settle on a modest plantation near Woodville. An older brother, Joseph E. Davis, rose to wealth and prominence, and he became a patron to young Jefferson. At the age of seven the lad was sent to St. Thomas College in Kentucky, but when he expressed a hope of becoming a Catholic priest like his teachers there, he was brought home for education locally. At the age of thirteen he was enrolled at Transylvania University, there studying math, surveying, Greek, Latin, history, and philosophy. However, his studies there were interrupted in 1824 when he was appointed to the United States Military Academy, from which he graduated in 1828. Posted as a second lieutenant to Wisconsin, he fought in the Black Hawk War and courted the daughter of his commanding officer, Colonel Zachary Taylor. "Old Rough and Ready" disapproved of the young man, but Sarah Knox Taylor spurned her father's advice and fled to the home of an aunt in Kentucky; Davis resigned his commission on June 30, 1835, and followed, and the two were married. They moved to Mississippi where Davis acquired a plantation, but within three months Sarah was dead of malaria.

During the next ten years Davis was a planter, staying close to his land except for occasional travels. In 1845, however, he was

Jefferson Davis, the Secretary of War who pushed Congress to appropriate money for the camel experiment. *Courtesy U. S. Signal Corps (Brady Collection), National Archives.*

elected to the House of Representatives, and he married Varina Howell, a local aristocrat. Hardly had he arrived in Washington than the Mexican War began, whereupon he resigned to command a regiment of "Mississippi Rifles." With them he fought at Monterrey and Buena Vista under the leadership of his former father-in-law, Zachary Taylor. Returning home a hero in 1847 as a result of his bravery at the Battle of Buena Vista, Davis was named a United States senator from Mississippi. During the next three years he served his state and the Democratic party, supporting the annexation of Mexican territory and opposing the entry of California as a free state. A commanding figure at this time, Davis was tall, erect, aristocratic; Carl Shurz, who heard Davis deliver a speech in the Senate, wrote, ". . . I was struck by the dignity of his bearing, the grace of his diction, and the rare charm of his voice—things which greatly distinguished him from many of his colleagues." [3] An ardent expansionist, he was ready as a senator to support any experiment that would make the West more accessible. Thus when Wayne talked of using camels as a means of exploring, mapping, and supplying the West, more especially the Southwest, Davis listened—and agreed. As chairman of the Senate committee on military affairs, he regularly urged an appropriation for this purpose.

However, in 1851 Davis resigned his seat in the Senate to return to Mississippi to contest for the governorship. When he lost this race, he retired to his plantation to resume the life of a planter. [4] Late in 1852, just as Davis' friend Franklin Pierce was winning the presidency, another advocate of importing camels came to the fore. George R. Gliddon, who for twenty-three years lived in the Middle East, eight of them as American consul at Cairo, suggested to the Senate committee on military affairs that it import fifty camels of different breeds for experiments in the West. Gliddon also recommended that ten Arabian handlers "familiar with their habits" should be imported for a period of two years to teach soldiers how to handle the beasts. From his travels across North Africa, Gliddon stated that camels could be found in great numbers along the coast of Africa, but that these were inferior to those to be found in the interior; therefore he recommended that the officer dispatched to purchase camels should travel to Nubia in the interior to secure them.[5] Nothing came of Gliddon's proposal, however.

Just at this point Jefferson Davis accepted the cabinet position of secretary of war at the request of President-elect Pierce. On March 7, 1853, he took the oath of office, thereby placing himself in a position to make an official recommendation concerning the use of camels. To guide him in drafting this recommendation, he asked that Wayne draft a statement about the beasts. The major did more than asked, for his letter of November 21 began with an examination of the geography of the West, noting that these 2,000,000 square miles were "without navigable Streams" and that any railroad built across the area would serve but a fraction thereof. By 1853, Wayne noted, "Communication with the interior of our Continent and throughout its centre is rare, and carried on slowly, and expensively by means of wagons drawn by horses, mules, or oxen, averaging on long journeys not more than twelve miles a day." And added to the cost of teams, harness, and wagons was the "continuous expenditure for teamsters, forage, shoes and repairs." With camels, he argued, there would be no need for wagons, little investment in harness, few teamsters required, and "almost nothing [required] for forage," yet "we can double the average of our daily journeys."

Warming to his task, Wayne noted that camels were used in parts of the world with climates similar to all of those found in the United States. Among the beast's good qualities, he noted that it lived to "a considerable age" and that it possessed "great strength, and astonishing powers of abstinence from food and drink. One draught of water will last it for several days—say three or four—whilst a few beans, a little meal, or the dry herbage and plants by the wayside, served it for food." As a beast of burden, "it will carry for short distances from 700 to 1200 pounds, accomplishing easily day after day, from 30 to 40 miles. Of the Swiftness of the Dromedary, many wonderful stories are told—it is safe to say that it will easily accomplish on level ground, for several successive days, an average of a hundred miles a day." Nor would the camel suffer from tender feet due to the

A dromedary from Lower Egypt dressed in his finery. Drawing by Gwinn Harris Heap.

rocky terrain to be found in the West, Wayne argued, for the camel regularly traversed similar geography in Africa and Asia.

Wayne did more than make recommendations concerning the use of the camel as a beast of burden. He also inserted comments that greatly intrigued Jefferson Davis and that ultimately did much to undermine the experiment that followed, writing of uses of the camel for "Military purposes other than those of burden— as for Expresses, the pursuit of Marauders &c." He noted that the use of dromedaries would allow "speedy communication from point to point," allow rapid surveying, and give "the power of controlling the Indians by checking and promptly punishing their aggressions." On this score he noted that Napoleon had used a "Dromedary Corps . . . which partook of the nature of both Cavalry and Infantry *without the inconveniences of either.*" [6]

Davis, in his annual report as secretary of war, dated December 1, 1853, generally followed Wayne's argument. He wrote that the modes of transport then in use were so expensive "as to prompt inquiry for means which may be attained with better results." He concluded:

On the older continents, in regions reaching from the torrid to the frozen zone, embracing arid plains and precipitous mountains covered with snow, camels are used, with the best results. They are the means of transportation and communication in the immense commercial intercourse with central Asia. From the mountains of Circassia to the plains of India they have been used for various military purposes—to transmit despatches, to transport supplies, to draw ordnance, and as a substitute for the dragoon horse.

Napoleon when in Egypt used with marked success the dromedary, a fleet variety of the same animal, in subduing the Arabs, whose habits and country were very similar to those of the mounted Indians of our western plains. . . . For like military purposes, for expresses, and for reconnoissances, it is believed, the dromedary would supply a want now seriously felt in our service; and for transportation with troops rapidly moving across the country, the camel, it is believed, would remove an obstacle which now serves greatly to diminish the value and efficiency of our troops on the western frontier.

For these considerations it is respectfully submitted that the necessary provision be made for the introduction of a sufficient number of both varieties of this animal, to test its value and efficiency to our country and our service.[7]

Despite Davis' recommendation, neither house of Congress was inclined to appropriate money for the experiment. Yet the idea had become public, and gradually a large segment of the population seemed enamored of the idea. By 1854 several of the largest newspapers in the country were carrying stories about the virtues of the beast, scholarly books were appearing in print urging their importation, and distinguished lecturers were addressing themselves to the subject. That year Gwinn Harris Heap published a journal of a trip he and Edward Fitzgerald Beale had taken the previous year from Missouri to California, and in an appendix he stated his strong belief that the camel would serve with distinction in the Southwest. Heap was the son of Samuel Davis Heap, who had served for many years as American consul at Tunis, and there he had studied the camel closely; thus his comments carried weight—and authority.[8]

That same year of 1854 John Russell Bartlett, recently returned from his travels in the Southwest as American Commissioner on the Joint Boundary Commission surveying the line dividing the United States and Mexico, published two large volumes about his travels. In this *Personal Narrative*, he wrote that "in traversing the broad plains and deserts of the interior of the continent, the subject of using camels as a means of transportation occurred to me." Bartlett, a Rhode Island scholar never hesitant to puff and posture himself, declared authoritatively, "From my experience of nearly three years with horses, mules, asses, and oxen, and with wagons, carts, and packs, I do not hesitate to hazard the opinion, that the introduction of camels and dromedaries would prove an immense benefit to our present means of transportation, that they would be a great saving to animal life, and would present facilities for crossing our broad deserts and prairies not possessed by any other domestic animals now in use." He argued that the camel could adapt to any climate known in the United States, that the beast would find mesquite beans to his liking and would thrive on them, and that it could carry large burdens economically.[9]

In the fall of that same year of 1854, George Perkins Marsh began delivering a series of lectures at the Smithsonian Institution. A distinguished scientist, traveler, and diplomat, Marsh commented in his introductory lecture that he spoke from knowledge gained through "residence of some years in the Turkish empire," as well as "several months of travel in Egypt, Nubia, Arabia Petraea and Syria." After gathering as much information about camels as he could through "inquiry and correspondence," he consulted "the books of travel and natural history to which I had access." These led him to "a strong persuasion of the probable success of a judiciously conducted attempt to naturalize in the new world this oldest of domestic quadrupeds." Marsh felt that the camel would prove valuable in two areas: as a beast of burden to carry supplies, and as an animal of war. He then appended a chapter entitled "Military Uses of the Camel" in which he reviewed the historic success of armies mounted on camels.[10]

One novelist, Joseph Warren Fabens, had stimulated popular interest in camels by publishing in 1851 a novel, *The Camel Hunt*, in which he chronicled the imaginary adventures of an American expedition sent to Algeria to secure camels for use in California.[11] So widespread had talk of using camels become that by the early 1850s some businessmen saw in the beasts a potential for profit. On August 4, 1853, W. G. Snethen wrote Secretary of War Jefferson Davis asking, on behalf of a client, if the War Department "would feel justified, under existing laws, to entertain a proposition to enter into a contract for a limited time, for the transportation of War and Military Stores, by *means of the camel,* across the continent from Corpus Christi, by way of the Gila route, to San Francisco, on terms *better than now paid* by the Government for similar transportation across the Isthmus—*each trip out, to be made within twenty days from the time of starting.*" If the answer was affirmative, Snethean stated that a bid shortly would be submitted by a responsible company. He said that the parties involved were "not actuated by the mere profits of the adventure, but rather by a desire to test the question, whether the *camel* would not be the *cheapest, swiftest, & most enduring burden-bearer* for the Plateau between the Atlantic & Pacific."

Davis replied affirmatively on August 17, whereupon Snethen responded with a request to Quartermaster General Thomas Jesup to quote the "prices which were paid last year by the Department, of which you are the head, for the transportation of munitions and stores between Indianola by way of San Antonio & also by the way of Cape Horn to San Diego thence to Ft. Yuma." He also requested to know the amount of *"time required*—under present arrangements of the Department—for transportation of munitions & stores, between any principal northern Entrepot on the Atlantic Coast—say New York—& San Diego," as well as the time required to transport goods from New Orleans to San Antonio and El Paso. Finally he wished some estimate of the amount of goods to be moved each year.

Snethen, receiving the requested information, submitted the bid of his clients, "C. W. Weber, for Himself and others," on October 5, 1853. Involved were three proposed routes: from Indianola to El Paso by way of San Antonio, each camel to carry 1000 pounds of freight and to travel thirty-three miles a day, the trip to be made in not more than thirty days, and the cost to be "ten cents per pound gross for the single trip, and Eighty Dollars the single trip, for each man the Government may have to transport"; from San Diego to Fort Yuma, each camel to carry 500 pounds and to travel eighty miles a day, the trip to be made in three days, and the rate of pay to be ten cents a pound and fifty dollars for each man transported; and the third a two-year contract to transport all government stores except heavy ordnance from San Diego to Fort Yuma, each camel to carry 1000 pounds and travel thirty-three miles a day, the trip to be made each way in seven days, and the cost five cents a pound for freight and twenty-five dollars per man.[12]

Apparently nothing came of this proposal, for no contracts were let. Preserved with these letters, however, is a prospectus issued by the "Camel Transportation Company" of New York City soliciting an investment of $30,000 from investors. "The object of this Company," stated the prospectus, "is to import one hundred Camels" to be employed between Corpus Christi and San Francisco "for the transportation of passengers, baggage, gold dust, mails, &c.," and across the Isthmus between Chagres and Panama City "for the same purposes." The estimated cost of this venture was $32,000. However, it noted that on the first round trip from Corpus Christi to San Francisco the entire investment would be recovered. With twenty camels held in reserve, eighty camels, each carrying a passenger plus 200 pounds of baggage at a cost of $100, would net $8000; on the return trip the eighty camels, each carrying a passenger plus baggage at a cost of $300, would net $24,000. This, said the prospectus, was "perhaps the least profitable route" over which to use camels. Yet the profit to be expected was not the most important aspect of the enterprise, this advertisement noted. More important would be the inevitable acceptance of camels by the Army for use against the Indians: "It will be perceived, that the running camel and dromedary moves with ease for weeks together, at the rate of eighty miles a day, while no horse can go longer than one day to a day and a half at the same rate; they are evidently the only animals upon which we can undertake to outstrip and subdue the border tribes." Thus potential investors would be making a profit while contributing to a patriotic undertaking.[13]

This venture also came to naught, but so firmly was public opinion swinging in favor of these animals that in 1854 a group of merchants in New York City organized and incorporated the American Camel Company. That year the company secured a charter from the state of New York; the stated purpose of the company was to import the animals and use them for trade and travel in the West. Again, nothing resulted.[14]

Secretary of War Jefferson Davis was aware that public attention had been focused on camels and that the public attitude generally seemed favorable. Thus in his second annual message to the President, reporting on his department, he renewed his request for funds: "I again invite attention to the advantages to be anticipated from the use of camels and dromedaries for military and other purposes, and, for the reasons set forth in my last annual report, recommend that an appropriation be made to introduce a small number of the several varieties of this animal, to test their adaptation to our country." [15]

Despite Davis' second recommendation, members of the House appropriations committee and the committee on military affairs did not include funds for the purpose in the original draft of the appropriations bill for fiscal year 1856. However, one member of the House, James Alexander McDougall of California, on December 27, 1854, recommended an amendment to the bill, one which would set aside $20,000 to be used by the secretary of war to import camels and dromedaries. Other members were not enthusiastic, and the appropriations bill went to the Senate without McDougall's recommendation.[16]

In the upper house, however, Seanator James Shields of Ohio on January 24, 1855, proposed adding Section 4 to the bill: "That the sum of thirty thousand dollars be and the same is hereby appropriated to be expended under the direction of the War Department, in the purchase and importation of camels and dromedaries to be employed for military purposes." Significantly Shields omitted from his amendment that part of Jefferson Davis' recommendation that camels be imported "for military *and other* purposes" [italics added]. A philosophical division was beginning, one that would haunt the experiment later. The other Senators knew nothing of this, however, and accepted the amendment without a dissenting vote.[17]

The Senate's amended version of the bill appropriating money for the War Department was then returned to the House for concurrence or rejection. In the lower chamber Congressman John Smith Phelps of Missouri on March 1 moved acceptance of the same amendment added by Senator Shields, but with the addition of two commas. The only discussion originated with Congressman Alfred B. Greenwood of Arkansas, who took the floor to voice a question:

> I desire to make an inquiry of the gentleman from Missouri, [Mr. Phelps], who has charge of this bill. I wish to know whether the Secretary of War would have the power, under the provisions of the amendment, to import Arabs into this country to take care of the dromedaries? They do not understand our language, and it would seem useless to bring them here.

Phelps responded, "I was about to say that the Committee on Ways and Means recommended a concurrence with this amendment; but I have no desire to enter into any explanation of it. The Secretary of War is in favor of introducing dromedaries, for the purpose of testing the use of them upon the plains." [18]

Apparently this brief response satisfied everyone in the House—and ultimately the Senate—for the amendment carried unanimously, emerging as Section 4 of Public Law LXX, the act appropriating funds for the Army for the period July 1, 1855, to June 30, 1856. The act was signed into law on March 3, 1855.[19]

Davis moved swiftly to carry the scheme into reality. First, of course, he sent an officer to purchase camels and see to their transport to the United States. Inasmuch as this would require the use of a ship, the secretary of war turned to his counterpart, the secretary of the navy,[20] for assistance. To his joy, Davis learned that the storeship *Supply* was to embark on or about May

20, 1855, for the Mediterranean; there it was to rendezvous with an American squadron of ships at "Spezzia" (La Spezia, Italy) and deliver supplies. The secretary of the navy agreed that after the *Supply* had fulfilled this mission, it could be made available for the purpose of securing camels.

The *Supply* had been built in 1846 at Medford, Massachusetts, on order by William Goddard, a merchant from Boston. However, in December that year the vessel was purchased by the United States Navy for use as a storeship for $60,000. The original name *Crusader* was changed to *Supply* at that time. Constructed of wood and powered only by sails, the ship was 141 feet long, twenty-nine feet wide, and had a depth of twenty-one feet. With two decks and three masts, it had a tonnage of 547 tons and an average speed of five knots. For protection it carried four twenty-four pounders. During the Mexican War the vessel was used by the Home Squadron operating in the Gulf of Mexico, after which it had sailed the Mediterranean and the Pacific, even accompanying Commodore Perry's expedition to Japan in 1853–1855.[21]

Davis looked no farther than Major Henry C. Wayne in seeking an Army officer to direct what was designated the Camel Military Corps. Naturally he also wanted a Naval officer sympathetic to the project in command of the *Supply*, and for advice on this score he listened to a friend he recently had made—a former lieutenant in the Navy and a camel enthusiast—Edward Fitzgerald Beale.

Few men in the vicinity of Washington, D.C., in the spring of 1855 had led a more unusual life than Beale. Born on February 4, 1822, in the District of Columbia, Beale was a "Navy brat." His father, George Beale, was paymaster for the Navy and had won the Congressional Medal of Honor during the War of 1812 for his bravery during the Battle of Lake Champlain, while his maternal grandfather had been a famous commodore. While studying at Georgetown University, he received an appointment from President Andrew Jackson to the Naval Academy. Graduating from that institution in 1842, he accepted a commission and went on active duty. During the Mexican War, he brought dispatches

The *U. S. S. Supply,* the ship which transported the camels to Texas. *Courtesy Library of Congress.*

from Commodore Robert F. Stockton of the Pacific Squadron to Washington, then returned to join in the fighting in California. There he was detached to service ashore, joining the forces of General Stephen Watts Kearny at the Battle of San Pascual. On February 9, 1847, he was sent overland, with Kit Carson, to carry dispatches to Washington about the victory, arriving there in June. During the next two years he made six trips from East Coast to West, carrying dispatches as a government courier. On one of these trips, made in 1848, he brought the first gold from California to Washington, confirming the rumors of a great discovery which had been circulating. He married Mary Edwards of Chester, Pennsylvania, in the summer of 1849, and he resigned from the navy two years later to become manager of large land holdings in California belonging to W. H. Aspinwall and Commodore Stockton.

In 1852, however, he returned to Washington where he was appointed superintendent of Indian Affairs for California and Nevada. Thereupon he began lobbying for an appropriation of

$25,000 from Congress to improve the condition of the natives under his supervision, and received this in March of 1853. With Gwinn Harris Heap, to whom he was related, he set out in May to go overland from Missouri to California (Heap, as noted earlier, published the journal he kept of this trip).

While on these various treks back and forth across the continent, Beale had become convinced that camels could be used effectively in the West. This idea first occurred to him when he and Kit Carson were exploring Death Valley. Later it was reinforced from his reading of Abbe Evariste R. Huc's *Recollections of a journey through Tartary, Thibet, and China, during the years 1844, 1845 and 1846,* published in New York in 1852. When Congress finally appropriated funds for the camel experiment in March of 1855, Beale was vacationing in Chester, Pennsylvania, and heard of it.[22] Immediately he urged another of his relatives, a lieutenant in the navy named David Dixon Porter, to apply for command of the ship sent to secure the camels. Porter, a brother-in-law of Gwinn Harris Heap, liked the idea and made known his desire to the secretary of the navy and secretary of war. Also, Beale wrote letters of recommendation, and both men were pleased when the appointment was made.

Porter was well qualified to undertake command of this mission. He had been born in Chester, Pennsylvania, on June 8, 1813, to a naval family. After a scant formal education, he went to sea at ten, sailing with his father to the West Indies; three years later he again went with his father, this time to Mexico. There he entered the Mexican Navy as a midshipman, sailing aboard the *Esmeralda* at a time when Spain was still trying to reconquer its lost colony of Mexico. Later, aboard the *Guerrero,* he participated in a fierce battle with the Spanish frigate *Lealtad.* Taken captive, he was imprisoned at Havana until his release early in 1829. Returning home, he was appointed a midshipman in the United States Navy on February 2, 1829. There followed a cruise of two years in the Mediterranean aboard the *Constellation,* a brief leave home, and then two more years in the Mediterranean. On that second trip, made aboard the *United States,* he courted and won the hand of George Ann Patterson, daughter of the commodore commanding the ship. They married on March 10, 1839.

David D. Porter. *Courtesy U. S. Signal Corps (Brady Collection), National Archives.*

Beginning in 1835, Porter was assigned to the Coast Survey, working off the Atlantic Coast and in Washington. In 1841, after achieving the rank of lieutenant, he sailed aboard the *Congress* in the Mediterranean and off the coast of Brazil. During the war with Mexico, as a first lieutenant, he served with the Home Squadron in the Gulf, seeing war firsthand at Vera Cruz and at Tabasco; Commodore Matthew Perry praised him as a "brave and zealous officer." However, after the war he was returned to Washington for duty with the Naval Observatory. Finding this monotonous, he took a leave of absence to command merchant vessels, sailing around the tip of South America, to Havana and Chagres, and to Melbourne and Sydney. Such was his status in the spring of 1855 when he was home on leave and talked with Edward Fitzgerald Beale about the camel experiment. Reinstated a lieutenant in the Navy, he was given command of the *Supply*. [23]

On May 10, 1855, Secretary of War Davis sent orders to Major Wayne, instructing him to "proceed without delay to the Levant" in order to "execute the law of the Congress." Davis noted that in order to purchase the camels Wayne—and Porter, "who has been associated with you in the commission"—might find it necessary to journey to the interior of "Asia" and there might chance upon governments with which the United States had no diplomatic relations; in such cases the two "will present yourselves in your official capacities, as charged by your government with a special commission, and request, in the name of your government, such friendly offices as international courtesy warrants."

On their way to the Middle East, the two were to stop in England and France to consult with persons having knowledge of the camel. Davis concluded, ". . . It is hardly necessary to mention, but still I do so to impress it upon you, that time is an important element, and that I wish you to be as prompt in the execution of this duty as the security of the experiment will permit, to which, of course, everything else must be subordinate." [24]

Six days later Davis sent "instructions" for "guidance" to Lieutenant Porter, who, although not an officer in the Army, nevertheless had been detailed by the secretary of the navy to cooperate in the project to import camels. Next he noted that Major Wayne already had departed for Europe to obtain information about camels from officers in several countries, but then would join Porter at La Spezia. Then the two were to go to Smyrna, next to Salonica, thence to Constantinople "provided there are no serious obstacles in the way, owing to the war in that quarter," [25] and through the Dardanelles into the Black Sea. Davis obviously had been soliciting information about camels, for he wrote, "It is believed that the best breed of camels is to be found in Persia; and as nothing should be left undone to procure the very best for our purposes, you may find it necessary to take your ship to the nearest point of communication with that country, when Major Wayne and yourself can set out on an expedition inland." Should Porter find it impossible to go through the Dardanelles into the Black Sea: "take your ship to the coast of Syria and disembark the land expedition at Beyrout [Beruit] or such other point as may be most suitable for the purpose."

Two things stood out in Davis' instructions: procure both varieties of camels, and "Whenever you meet with fine animals it would be well to procure them." Once the camels were aboard ship, Porter was to return during "the most suitable season of the year" to the coast of Texas, landing them at the "most convenient point" there. Once the beasts came ashore in Texas, Major Wayne or some other person designated by the secretary of war would "take sole charge of them." Porter then was to return to New York unless instructed otherwise.

As a precaution against accident, Davis included for Porter a copy of his previous instructions to Wayne and noted that, in case Wayne became incapacitated in any way, Porter was to "proceed alone to fulfill [sic] these instructions." [26]

The two men, Wayne and Porter, met in New York City on May 18 and together inspected the *Supply*. They also discussed the type of arms and ammunition they might need when they journeyed inland in search of camels, and what medicines they might require for man and camel. Moreover, they took measure of one another; Wayne that same day wrote Jefferson Davis, "You know already my estimate of Lieutenant Porter's abilities, but I must add that, in the completeness and thoroughness of the details, he has far exceeded my most sanguine expectatvons." [27]

Wayne concluded his report by stating that he was to sail the next day, May 19, at noon for Southampton, England, aboard the *Hermann*, a merchant vessel. During the hours yet remaining to him in the United States, he visited with his family—and decided to take his oldest son, eleven-year-old Henry Nicholl, with him on the journey.[28]

Photograph of Henry C. Wayne and his two sons, Henry Nicholl (left) and James Moore, taken in May of 1855 just before he sailed for England. *Courtesy Library of Congress.*

Fifteen days later he was in England, reporting to Davis on June 7 that he had deposited £4000 with George Peabody and Company and that he had made a courtesy call on the U.S. minister to England, James Buchanan. Through Buchanan's aid he was able to converse with various scientists at the Royal College of Surgeons, the Zoological Society, and the Zoological Gardens. Everywhere he was assured that the camel could be acclimatized to the United States, and at the Zoological Society he was allowed to study the feeding, care, and hygiene of camels. Enthusiastically, Wayne concluded, ". . . The result of my researches . . . in England, may be summed up in a few words, as follows: that the camel stands well the climate of London; that it breeds in it; and that a European can manage the animal as well as an Arab." [29]

Next Wayne and his son traveled to Paris, arriving there on June 20. Again he conversed with gentlemen of science, but the French he found pessimistic about the chances of success with camels in the United States. However, noted Wayne, their views stemmed from their knowledge of only the camels of Africa. Disappointed at what he found in France, he enjoyed himself with his son by visiting places of interest to the boy. Then, apparently changing his mind about how the lad would fare during the rest of the trip, he placed young Henry Nicholl in a French school and on July 17 left for Pisa, Italy, via Marseilles. He would not see his son again until the lad returned to New York more than three years later.[30]

While in Genoa, en route to Pisa, Wayne received a letter from Lieutenant Porter stating that the *Supply* had arrived at La Spezia and that while the ship was being unloaded he would inspect the camels at Pisa. Therefore Wayne had no reason to continue to Pisa; instead he journeyed directly to La Spezia, arriving there on the morning of July 24. A few hours later Porter returned from Pisa, [31] and the two no doubt compared experiences since last they had met in New York City.

Porter on May 23 had received his final orders from the Navy. He was to sail the *Supply* to La Spezia, deliver his stores, and then carry out the orders of the secretary of war. Should he come into contact with some senior officer, he was to show his orders, which specifically stated that he was to have no interference "except in a case of great emergency." And all senior officers were authorized to afford Porter assistance in carrying out the mission of procuring camels.[32] Porter sailed from New York on June 3, going directly to La Spezia. There he had left the ship to journey to Pisa, where camels reportedly could be viewed, but he learned little about the camel there.

On July 25, both officers aboard the *Supply*, they set sail for Naples. Porter wanted to halt there briefly to convert the American currency he had for purchasing supplies along the way into coins that would be readily accepted in the Mediterranean area. He had been told that the rate of exchange in Naples was most favorable, but three days later when they arrived at that Italian city they found the reverse to be true. Therefore they decided to postpone this financial transaction until they got to Malta. Meanwhile the two officers had determined to sail next to Tunis. There they intended to procure a camel "for the purpose of studying the animal and its management on shipboard." [33]

They arrived in Tunis on the afternoon of August 4, and there they were joined by Gwinn Harris Heap, Porter's brother-in-law. Heap's father had died in Tunis in October 1853, just as Heap and Beale were completing their trek from Missouri to California; immediately he had returned to Tunis and was still there when the *Supply* arrived in August 1855. Happily he joined the expedition—and proved a valuable addition. Because of his long residence in the Middle East, he was thoroughly familiar with camels, and he spoke some of the languages of that region. In addition, he was a passing-fair artist and would draw the sketches that would accompany Wayne's report of the expedition. His salary was set at $130 per month plus expenses.[34]

The three men must have visited happily, bubbling with excitement now that the procuring of camels was about to begin. Heap had been enthusiastic on the subject of using camels in the American West for three years and had written about the prospect, while Wayne had advocated the project for almost a decade. Now they were anchored in the Gulf of Tunis and could look out across the water to the buildings of the town. Breezes from inland brought exotic, foreign smells, while occasionally they could glimpse something that might be a camel moving. The three men knew that at last they were taking the first step to make the camel experiment a reality.

3
BRINGING
CAMELS
TO
AMERICA

Ambrose Bierce, the post-Civil War wit, who authored *The Devil's Dictionary*, defined the camel as "A quadruped (the *Splaypes humpidorus*) of great value to show business. There are two kinds of camels—the camel proper and the camel improper. It is the latter that is always exhibited." Although this was written many years after Major Henry C. Wayne, Lieutenant David D. Porter, and Gwinn Harris Heap arrived off the coast of Tunis on August 4, 1855, they gradually would come to appreciate the sentiment, for they were in search of the proper camel for use in the United States.

Their immediate task was to purchase one camel, bring it aboard the *Supply*, and study the animal while learning how to manage it on the ship. Because Porter was ill, Wayne went ashore alone and made the purchase. Then he stopped to visit with the American consul, W. P. Chandler, who suggested a courtesy call on the new bey of Tunis, Mohammed Pasha. After the two exchanged pleasantries, Wayne paused at the palace to request a permit from the minister of state to load the camel he had purchased. Mohammed Pasha, learning of this request, asked why the American wanted a camel. Wayne informed him of the experiment, whereupon the bey stated that he would send from his private herd an exceedingly fine beast. Wayne accepted the gift "in the name of the President and the people of the United States," thinking he then had a pair of camels. However, the next day, when the bey's gift arrived, there was not one but two camels, both stallions, one grown and the other young, making a total of three animals aboard. They were transferred to the ship without incident and stored between decks.[1]

On August 10 the ship sailed for Malta. During the voyage Wayne and Porter watched closely to see how the three camels were adapting to life aboard ship. Surprisingly the beasts proved good travelers, giving "very little trouble, very much less than a horse would," wrote Porter. However, the camel originally purchased by Wayne quickly developed an itch, a disease to which the animal is particularly liable; they applied the same medicine generally used on horses and cows and found it worked well enough. Wayne was convinced that by currying, brushing, and cleaning the camels, further outbreaks of itch could be prevented,

A dromedary on the move across the desert as drawn by Gwinn Harris Heap.

and therefore he contracted with two sailors aboard to perform these chores, for "a small additional compensation," on the three animals. By observing the beasts, Wayne learned that they ate eight to twelve pounds of hay daily plux six quarts of oats, and drank on the average two and a half to three buckets of water every three days. He concluded that "Americans will be able to manage camels not only as well, but better than Arabs, as they will do it with more humanity and with far greater intelligence." [2]

From Malta the *Supply* sailed first to Smyrna (present Izmir, Turkey), then to Salonika (Thessalonika, Greece), and arrived at Constantinople on October 4. Wayne had converted his American dollars to silver, $10,000 of it, at Malta, for he needed currency readily acceptable in the countries he would visit. During this time the two men were learning that camels were scarce in 1855 throughout the region because of the Crimean War then in progress; the British government had just contracted for 8000 camels for use by its forces, these in addition to those they had purchased the year before. As a result the price of camels had risen to forty to fifty dollars for good females nad seventy-five to one hundred dollars for the best males.

Leaving the *Supply* at Constantinople, Wayne and Porter traveled by British ship to Balaklava, landing in the Crimea on the seventeenth. There, courtesy of the British Army, they observed both the Bactrian (two-humped) and the Arabian (one-humped) camels in military usage. Wayne observed that the Bactrian camel presented special difficulties in loading because of the formation of its back, but that it was capable of carrying immense burdens. Most Britishers, he noted, preferred the Arabian species, saying it was more serviceable; during the war the one-humped camel had carried army burdens of 600 pounds apiece for an average of twenty-five to thirty miles a day. Those simply ridden by soldiers were capable of journeying seventy miles daily. [3]

The two returned to Constantinople without purchasing any additional camels. There they disposed of two of the animals they had acquired in Tunis, the one purchased by Wayne and the younger one presented by the bey. One had suffered a recurrence

The Bactrian camel as drawn by Gwinn Harris Heap.

of the itch, while the other, said Porter, was "rather an ordinary specimen, not worth taking to the United States." The Sultan of Turkey, hearing of their visit, offered to present them with four beasts from his private herd but would have to send to the interior for them. Wayne and Porter decided their time was too short to wait and sailed without them, bound for Alexandria, Egypt. They arrived there on November 29, only to learn that the American consul was in Cairo.

Major Wayne decided to journey there and was accompanied by Heap. The two, in company with an American naval officer, therefore set out on December 7, reaching Cairo the following day. Camels were readily available in that city—Wayne found he could purchase as many as he wanted—but the government of the country banned the export of the animals. And Wayne and Edwin De Leon, the American consul, quarreled to the point where De Leon became offended and departed for Alexandria. However, with the aid of C. Kahil, the American vice-consul at Cairo, Wayne and Heap secured an audience with Zoulfokhar Pacha, the minister of finance and confidential secretary to the viceroy, during which the American major requested permission to export twenty camels. Pacha, by letter on December 24, gave the viceroy's reply: "That it is contrary to the custom of the country to permit the exportation of animals to foreign countries, but that, out of regard to the American government, he gives his permission for the purchase of two camels, only, and that the necessary instructions have been given to the governor of Alexandria to permit their exportation." [4]

Wayne protested that, while he was pleased that the viceroy held good will for the government of the United States, he needed more camels, that his mission was scientific in nature, that the voyage to the United States would be tedious and that some animals might die, and that he therefore needed additional animals. The next day, December 25, Pacha replied that the viceroy would allow two male and two female camels to be exported. Wayne thereupon purchased five camels and sent them ahead to Alexandria, thinking the viceroy would relent and allow the additional beast to be taken aboard the *Supply*. He then journeyed back to Alexandria, arriving there on December 30.

At this point Wayne and Edwin De Leon, the consul, apparently began working together again. De Leon requested two Minie rifles and ammunition as a present for the viceroy, who also had arrived in Alexandria; Wayne added a bullet mold, and they were given to His Highness. The result was a change of heart by the viceroy; on January 21 there arrived on the docks six "young, sound and healthy" dromedaries, although, noted Wayne, they were "all of the common stock." Meanwhile, two of the five beasts which Wayne purchased in Cairo "exhibited evidences of the itch," and he chose to sell them rather than run the risk of their infecting the whole herd. Therefore when the *Supply* sailed on January 22, Porter had on board the six animals presented by the viceroy, three of the beasts purchased by Wayne in Cairo, and the one given them by the Bey of Tunis, a total of ten.[5]

While in Egypt the Americans purchasing camels watched carefully to see how the animals were employed there; this drawing, which Major Wayne submitted with his report, was typical of what they saw.

The process devised by David D. Porter for loading the camels aboard the *Supply*. Drawing by Gwinn Harris Heap.

While the *Supply* was anchored at Alexandria waiting for Wayne to return from Cairo, Porter had discovered a major liability of the camel—the rutting season. Heap, from the ship, wrote Wayne on December 27, that Mohomet, the name given the animal presented them by the Bey of Tunis, was "in a high state of rut." Porter wanted to put the beast ashore until they were ready to sail, but Consul De Leon was unable or unwilling to secure the necessary permit for them.[6] Each year, they learned, the male is seized by the mating instinct, a "furious excitement" that lasts some three to four months. Female camels come into heat only for four or five days, but not necessarily every year. Thus the males become ungovernable, violent, nervous, and revengeful, biting without provocation—and the male is capable of biting off an arm or, more frequently, a kneecap. During this ordeal the male's eyes become inflamed, he foams at the mouth, and hardly tastes his food.[7]

Wayne, meanwhile, was learning to become more careful in dealing with the sellers of camels. Those people with animals for

A drawing of a burden camel in Egypt, submitted by Henry C. Wayne with his report to Secretary of War Jefferson Davis.

sale are the same worldwide: they love a greenhorn and will try, during their salespitch, to make the animal under consideration seem the best of his breed. With the camel, however, sellers went a step further. Inasmuch as the state of a dromedary's hump was a quick index to the state of the animal's health—a plump, solid one indicated a healthy beast, while a flaccid hump indicated one severely used—dishonest camel dealers resorted to various means to change the appearance of the animals they had for sale. A favorite means was to perforate the animal's skin, insert a reed, and blow up the hump until it assumed a look of plumpness and solidarity.[8]

On January 22, 1856, the *Supply* sailed for Smyrna. To care for the ten camels aboard, Wayne had hired three "Arabs" to aid the Americans already retained for this purpose. Before leaving the United States, Wayne had retained the services of Albert Ray as "wagon and forage master." Ray brought to the task a "general acquaintance with animals, their habits, and diseases." During the months since the first dromedary had been brought aboard, he had increased his knowledge by observation, care of the animals aboard, and reading the books furnished him by Wayne.[9]

While Wayne had still been in Cairo negotiating for an export license, Gwinn Harris Heap was journeying ahead to Smyrna by commercial steamer in order to purchase the remaining camels needed to fill the ship. When at last the *Supply* arrived there, he was waiting with the twenty-one animals he had secured: "four Arabian males, one cross of the Bactrian upon the Arabian, fifteen females, and a fine Bactrian that accidentally came into this part of the country." Wayne had not anticipated having a two-humped animal, but he approved Heap's actions because this would "enable us to carry to America one of that species without difficulty, though it will a little complicate the experiment, not, however, to any very objectionable degree." Some of the females were pregnant; indeed one of them gave birth a few nights after Wayne arrived. And all the females, as they came into heat, were bred—as Davis had instructed. The purpose, of course, was to see how well the camel might be adapted to America, and the perpetuation of the herd was a necessary ingredient.[10]

On February 2 a male Bactrian camel arrived in Smyrna from

Crossing the Bactrian and dromedary produced a hybrid camel known as a "Tuilu." Drawing by Gwinn Harris Heap.

the interior, and Wayne purchased it, bringing the herd to thirty-three. Porter thereupon announced that the *Supply* could not comfortably accommodate any more of the animals. All that remained was securing the necessary packsaddles and covers from local sources. Wayne wrote the secretary of war that within days he intended to sail for Texas and that he was confident the animals would prove easy passengers. Wagonmaster Ray, his American helpers, and three Arabs hired by Wayne would care for the beasts during the voyage; Major Wayne stated that these men would give constant attention to the camels to avoid injury and halt disease. However, to be certain that the animals were properly cared for, he engaged the services of "two Turks as camel conductors" in Smyrna.

And he reported with pride that of the $20,000 given to him in May of 1855 to be used for the purchase of camels, $12,000 was still in hand not expended.[11]

Three days later he sent another letter to Davis giving a full list of the animals he was bringing to Texas:

    1 Tunis camel of burden, male.
    1 Sennar dromedary, male.
    1 Muscat dromedary, female.
    2 Siout dromedaries, males.
    4 Siout dromedaries, females.
    1 Mount Sinai dromedary, male.
    2 Bactrian camels, male.
    1 "Booghdee" or "Tuilu," male (produce of the Bactrian male and
        Arabian female).
    4 Arabian camels of burden, males.
   15 Arabian camels of burden, females.
    1 Arabian camel 24 days old, male.

He indicated that he anticipated arriving off the coast of Texas sometime between April 15 and May 1, and asked that preparations be made for "lightering" the animals ashore; by this he meant that the beasts should be transferred from the *Supply* to smaller vessels while anchored in the harbor; the camels then would come ashore by means of the small ships. And he wanted a

The dromedary of Muscat, as drawn by Gwinn Harris Heap.

clean stable waiting ashore where the animals could recuperate from their long confinement aboard ship.[12]

Lieutenant Porter at this point indicated a flair for public relations, suggesting that after his cargo was unloaded on the coast of Texas he should be allowed to proceed to Washington, bringing with him a camel for exhibit to members of Congress. The result, he thought, would be "to induce Congress to grant another appropriation for the importation of camels." [13] Because of the danger that the animal might die and the result might be opposite of that desired the idea was abandoned.

The ship left Smyrna early on the morning of February 15 to be greeted by stormy weather in the Mediterranean. They passed the Rock of Gibraltar on March 5 to be greeted by even worse weather in the Atlantic. Three gales, two of them of severe intensity, made the passage a rough one. On April 13 they arrived at Kingston, Jamaica, and remained there six days. Then they sailed for Indianola, Texas, which they reached on April 29. Almost immediately upon sailing, two calves had been born, but owing to the intensity of the gale into which they were sailing the mother camels "apparently lost, through fear, all solicitude for their young," as Wayne phrased it; actually the calves died for want of nourishment, for the mothers would not rise to suckle them. The handlers tried to feed the calves a gruel of preserved milk and various combinations of other foods from the ship's stores, but this did not keep them alive. A female calf, born on February 27, thrived, however, and reached Texas. A fourth calf, born on March 19, did not fare so well; it died, Wayne reported, from fits produced by teething. Then on March 30 a female died attempting to give birth. Subsequently two more calves were born. One lived, and the other died when an adult laid upon it. The net result was six calves, four of them and one adult dead; therefore the *Supply* reached Texas with thirty-four passengers, one more than it began with.[14]

Lieutenant Porter, during this difficult voyage, tried every way possible to make the camels comfortable and healthy: "My plan," he wrote, "was to give them good food, and plenty of it; rub them thoroughly every day with currycomb and brush; keep every part

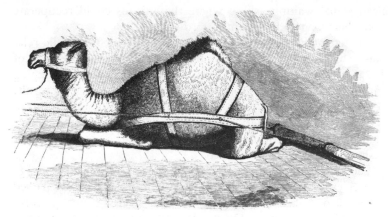

A drawing by Gwinn Harris Heap showing how camels were secured abroad the *Supply* during a storm at sea.

of their deck clean by scrubbing and whitewashing, and wash parts of their bodies every day with soap and water." Under this treatment, he asserted, the camels' health improved from what it had been when they were brought aboard—and Porter injected his private thoughts about the "ignorance and brutality" with which the Arabs, Egyptians, and Turks treated their animals. Before leaving New York in 1855, he had brought aboard ample stores of hay and oats, which he fed them liberally; although this differed from the camels' previous diet, they soon became accustomed to it and would, he said, "eat nothing else."

As to the itch, a disease to which camels seemed prone, Porter ordered it treated with sulphur externally and internally. This cured the itch in just three days. He reported that Egyptians attempted to cure the malady by smearing the animal all over with tar; he wryly observed that the medicine did cure the problem, but "not until the skin was almost taken off the body." Next Porter listed other camel cures employed by Egyptian "doctors." In Cairo a common medicine was to boil down a young sheep in molasses and then make the dromedary drink this "half scalding hot." Other cures included a chameleon's tail, with which the camel's nose was to be tickled; a piece of cheese forced down the dromedary would cure it of a cold; and an ounce of tea mixed with five grains of gunpowder would cure a camel with swollen legs. In the remainder of his report to Jefferson Davis, Porter wrote at length about the various measures he had employed to ensure the camels' safety, and he included recommendations for future procurement of the animals.[15]

Wayne occupied himself during the voyage arranging his report and compiling a series of documents about camels: a series of notes about the animal made by Linant de Bellefonds, a French engineer; a report from the agent at the estate of the son of a viceroy of Egypt; three letters from American missionaries in the Middle East giving their observations about dromedaries; notes about the beast by General L. L. Carbuccia, translated by Albert Ray; and a series of notes on the anatomy of dromedaries by General Carbuccia, translated by Dr. S. Allen Engles, a Navy doctor aboard the *Supply*.[16]

Gwinn Harris Heap was more visionary than the practical Lieutenant Porter or the scientific Major Wayne. An imaginative person, Heap spent his time devising a scheme to use camels to transmit mail and express material from several points in the Midwest to California and Oregon. He did this because he believed the camel superior to all forms of transport then in use except the railroad. He believed a camel mail express could be employed at a profit—and with great speed—between Corpus Christi, Texas, and Santa Fe, New Mexico; between Independence, Missouri, and Santa Fe; between Santa Fe and Salt Lake City; between Salt Lake City and Los Angeles; and from Independence to Los Angeles. On the latter route, he estimated the distance at 1878 miles and stated his belief that camels could cross it in twenty-eight days. He believed that sixty animals could cover this entire route, ten at each of the five terminals he had named, and ten extras. He concluded that the camel was a most admirable beast, for it was patient, not vicious, and lowered itself to the ground to be loaded and unloaded.[17]

The *Supply* dropped anchor at Powder Horn, three miles out

from Indianola, Texas, at 4:30 on the afternoon of April 29, 1856. Again the weather was unfavorable, and not until two days later could the *Fashion*, a lighter, come out to them. Still the swells were such that no camels could be transferred, and Wayne had to be content to go ashore on the small craft to post a notice of his arrival to Jefferson Davis; in this brief note he proudly noted the successful transport of camels from the Middle East to the United States, commenting, "I am happy to inform you that we have arrived, after an unusually rough passage, with one more camel than we started with." [18]

The next day, May 2, Wayne returned to the *Supply*, the *Fashion* bringing two schooners with it. One of the schooners came alongside the *Supply*, and the sailors aboard the Navy vessel loaded a camel aboard a sling to attempt a transfer. However, the *Supply* was moving so much from the high swell of the waves that the camel, suspended in mid air, began swinging and turning. Under such conditions Lieutenant Porter and the captain of the *Fashion* decided the transfer was unsafe for the animal and returned it to the *Supply*. Wayne concurred with this decision, not wanting to take his cargo of dromedaries safely from their original home to Texas only to injure them in unloading. Therefore he and Porter sailed to the mouth of the Mississippi, followed by the *Fashion*. [19] Inside the river's mouth, at Southwest Pass, the transfer was made safely from the *Supply* to the *Fashion*. The small vessel then returned to Indianola, arriving at Powder Horn at 11:30 a.m. By 8:00 that evening of May 14 all of the animals had been brought ashore successfully and stabled. [20] Porter later reported that he had delivered his cargo in good condition; only four showed any ill effect from the journey: "one with a bile on the leg, three with swollen feet from long confinement." Camels at last had come to the United States.

Jefferson Davis apparently was delighted with the success of the first voyage to secure camels, and, inasmuch as the original appropriation of $30,000 was far from expended, he decided to dispatch another expedition to acquire yet more of the animals. Accordingly he conferred with the secretary of the navy and requested the use of the *Supply* for this second mission; the permission secured, Davis wired Colonel D. D. Tompkins, the quartermaster at New Orleans, to inform Wayne that at the first opportunity the ship would be returning to the East. By letter he then asked if Wayne would like to make this second trip.

Major Wayne replied by letter on May 17 that he preferred "to continue with the camels already landed, and to carry out the remaining points of the experiment yet to be demonstrated, viz: acclimation and breeding." He made this decision because he did not want to leave the animals in the care of people unacquainted with camel habits and management, fearing that such would cause the failure of the experiment. Then in a second letter, he enclosed Heap's recommendations for the second voyage—and recommended that Heap be employed "as a suitable agent" should the secretary of war choose to hire a civilian to head the project.[21] With three of the foreign helpers hired to work with the camels, Wayne then busied himself in Texas after watching Porter and Gwinn Harris Heap sail for New York aboard the *Supply*. The vessel arrived safely at that port on May 28 whereupon Lieutenant Porter submitted his final report about his first voyage, concluding that he was awaiting further orders from the secretary of war.[22]

Davis, who was most eager to secure another shipload of animals to add to those already in Texas, moved rapidly. On June 18 he wrote Edwin De Leon, the American consul in Egypt, that Porter would be returning to that country and that Porter still had in his possession the permit issued by the viceroy allowing the export of ten dromedaries; this had not been utilized on the previous voyage because of the press of time. Davis wanted De Leon to get this permit renewed if possible; failing that, he was to try to get the viceroy's permission to drive ten camels from the interior across Egypt to board the *Supply* at Alexandria. Finally, he wanted De Leon to write Lieutenant Porter, who would be stopping at La Spezia, Italy, to inform him what the result of this request was; thereby Porter would not make a journey to Alexandria for nothing.[23]

Davis' instructions to Porter were direct. The lieutenant was to sail on the *Supply* to secure "an additional number of camels for the military service of the United States." If Consul De Leon secured a permit from the viceroy of Egypt to export camels from that country, he was to stop at Alexandria and procure the ten dromedaries, "the swift kind," then proceed to Smyrna to purchase "such specimens of the burden camel as seem best adapted to the soil and climate of the United States." Especially was he to attempt to purchase "fine animals of the Bactrian variety, and complete your list by selecting young camels of the approved crosses"; by this, Davis meant to secure hybrid breeds of camels.

To accomplish this task, Porter was to draw $10,000 from the Treasury Department, deposit this in a bank in New York, and draw letters of credit from that bank which would be negotiable abroad. If that plan did not seem suitable, he was to exchange the American dollars for French currency while in New York, for French currency was more negotiable in the Middle East than American money was. In addition, Porter was authorized to employ Gwinn Harris Heap at a salary of $2000 per year, plus expenses, to aid in this task.[24]

Accompanied by Heap, Lieutenant Porter sailed early in July with a load of naval stores for La Spezia, arriving there on September 11. Waiting there for the lieutenant was a letter from Consul De Leon, who had complied—somewhat—with the request of Jefferson Davis. He said that the permit secured from the viceroy earlier was given "as an act of international courtesy for this special occasion only," and therefore no longer was valid. Nor would De Leon request that it be renewed, for to do so would invite other nations to request export permits. Thus the original permit was useless. However, De Leon did report that the viceroy had given permission for camels to be transported through Egypt from the interior to the port of Alexandria; these could be secured from the "Sheiks of the Hedjaz [Hegas, Arabia]" at reasonable cost. In conclusion, De Leon wrote that the viceroy of Egypt recently had organized a dromedary corps of 480 camels, each carrying two soldiers and traveling thirty-five to sixty miles a day. He thought that Jefferson Davis, to whom the original copy of this letter was addressed, might be very interested in this successful use of the camel for military purposes.[25]

Egyptian dromedaries saddled for a trip. This drawing was submitted by
Henry C. Wayne with his report to Secretary of War Jefferson Davis.

Lieutenant Porter was far from impressed with what De Leon
had accomplished. He wrote Davis that a trip to Hegas would in-
volve a journey of 2000 miles and would require three months to
complete. To purchase ten camels from that area therefore would
require an expenditure of an estimated $7540, far too much to
secure only ten beasts. Moreover, there were hostile tribes in the
area, so that after the animals were purchased they probably
would be stolen. Therefore Porter concluded that he should go
directly to Smyrna, secure a load of animals there, and return
home.[26]

While the stores aboard the *Supply* were being unloaded at La
Spezia, Gwinn Harris Heap sailed by commercial vessel to
Smyrna to begin purchasing animals. That way no time would be
lost, for when Porter arrived with the vessel it could be loaded
immediately and the return voyage commence. On October 19 he
addressed a letter to Porter, his brother-in-law, that he had already secured twenty animals, and from a local sultan he had
received a gift of six additional dromedaries, bringing the total on

On the first and second expeditions to secure camels, Jefferson Davis was anxious that as many different types of animals as possible be secured; therefore Henry C. Wayne submitted with his report drawings of the various types of camels. This one is a dromedary from Lower Egypt; note the absence of a mane, which denotes that it is female.

hand to twenty-six. All were being held at the same corral used the year before on the previous trip. His intent was to journey into the interior to purchase an additional fourteen animals, but he hoped to return before Porter arrived. He hired an Italian "in whose intelligence I have no great reliance," but who came highly recommended by the American vice-consul; Heap noted in his letter to Porter that the Italian "drinks and has a weakness for the beau sexe. With all these faults he is the best person I could find, and such as he is, has nearly set me wild at times."

Also before his departure, Heap hired a local saddler to begin making packsaddles for the camels at a cost of $13.50 each, including saddle blanket. And he noted that the price of camels had increased since their visit the year before, although he felt those he had purchased were "a much finer lot than the last." [27]

His ship unloaded at last, Porter left La Spezia only to sail into "unprecedented bad weather." With the wind blowing directly against him, it took, at one point, twenty-one days to make only thirty-five miles. However, when he arrived at last at Smyrna, he was greeted by Heap, who had returned from the interior, his purchases completed. On hand were forty-four camels, "a beautiful lot of animals, all young (between three and four years old), and few of them have ever been under the saddle." These included two Bactrians, both male, three male Arabians, one male and one female cross between the Bactrian and the Arabian, and thirty-seven Arabian females. Many of the female camels were pregnant and due to give birth within four or five months. In addition, the saddle-maker had completed his work, so that everything was ready to be loaded.

Because of the greater number of animals than was carried the previous year, Porter found it necessary to make additional alterations on the *Supply*, but he had learned from his previous experience and thought the accommodations superior to those that had delivered thirty-four healthy camels to Texas. To care for the animals he hired nine additional men plus one boy on November 15, just before sailing. These men, hired "for the purpose of taking care of the camels on board the *Supply*, and to accompany them to their place of destination in Texas," were to receive fifteen dollars per month and they agreed to serve the government of the United States for at least six months if their services were needed. At the time of their discharge they were to receive an additional fifty dollars. Among these men were two who later would gain some fame in the Southwest, Hadji (or Hagis) Ali and George Caralambo.[28] Just before he departed a few days later, Porter wrote Davis that he anticipated arriving at the mouth of the Mississippi by January 20, 1857.[29]

Again he sailed into the face of bad weather. For thirteen days out of Smyrna Porter found it necessary to proceed under close-reefed topsails, "under water half the time, and officers and crew knocked up and worn out." He called these gales "the severest weather it has ever been my lot to meet with at sea." After fifteen days, during which time the lieutenant never was out of his clothing or touched his bed, he put in at Malta to rest. During this time the camels remained strapped down, but Porter proudly reported to Davis that not an accident had happened to them and all were "well and in fine condition." Therefore he stated that he did not anticipate keeping the schedule he earlier had forecast. And because he had been instructed to stop at Tangier to take on board the remains of the late consul he estimated he would not reach New Orleans until about February 10. However, he intended not to hurry, for he wanted to take the forty-four camels through in good shape. As to expenses on the voyage, he anticipated that there would be a surplus left from the $10,000 he had been given, even after Gwinn Harris Heap had been paid.[30]

Apparently the weather finally turned cooperative, for the *Supply* arrived at the mouth of the Mississippi on January 30, 1857, almost two weeks earlier than Porter previously had estimated. In his note to the secretary of war announcing his arrival, the lieutenant reported that on this voyage three of the camels had died, among them the two Bactrians: "one of them died suddenly in Malta, and the other two fell over dead, without a moment's warning, when eating their food and apparently in good health. There was no way of accounting for it, unless they swallowed something in their food; the first one, I think, died from fright, owing to the excessive motion of the ship, and would never eat afterwards." [31]

Waiting for him there was Albert Ray, still working as overseer of the camels. He had been sent to New Orleans with the steamer *Suwanee* to take the animals to Texas. During the next few days the forty-one surviving beasts were transferred to the small ship,

David D. Porter, a photograph taken during the Civil War era. *Courtesy U. S. Signal Corps (Brady Collection), National Archives.*

and it departed for Indianola. There on February 10 the forty-one were landed, all "in good order" according to Captain W. K. Van Bokkelen, the acting quartermaster.[32]

Once the camels were transferred off the *Supply*, Porter and Heap finished their reports, returned the vessel to New York, and settled their accounts with the government. Lieutenant Porter and Gwinn Harris Heap had completed their work. They were not the only ones to be severing their connection with the experiment. In national elections, held in November of 1856 while the *Supply* was anchored at Smyrna taking on camels, James Buchanan was elected President of the United States. Once in that office in March 1857, he picked his own cabinet—and Jefferson Davis was not among those men. Rather Buchanan chose John B. Floyd as secretary of war. Also terminating his work with the Camel Corps was Major Henry C. Wayne, who since the arrival of the first load of animals at Indianola the previous May had been experimenting with them near San Antonio.

4 EXPERIMENTS IN TEXAS

The arrival of the first load of camels at Indianola, Texas, on May 14, 1856, created a real stir among the local population—and an even greater reaction from local horses and mules. People crowded to the docks to see the strange animals imported from across the sea, most of them getting their first glimpse ever of a beast about which previously they had only read. At this port the national government had twenty-five wagons and teams on hand for hauling federal cargoes loading or unloading there. Fred Holz-heuser, a young German immigrant lad of thirteen employed to work with the horses, later recalled, "We had the government teams hitched up when the camels were brought ashore, and the teams ran away and upset the wagons. It took a long time to round-up and catch the teams." [1]

Major Henry C. Wayne, who had chosen to remain in Texas with the newly imported animals, learned a major lesson that day. Perhaps because he had been in such close proximity to camels for several months aboard ship, he might have overlooked something the horses did not: the dromedary has a peculiar, distinct, and strong odor. George Perkins Marsh, during his lectures at the Smithsonian, had addressed himself to this topic by quoting an experienced traveler in the Middle East, who wrote that the odor of a camel was not "more easily imagined than described. No; as there are heights to which imagination cannot soar, so are there depths to which it cannot descend. I remember one evening and night in Wadee Feiran. No water—thermometer at 110°, air deathly still, and camels *very* near. Oh, for a draught of Lethe [poison]! Reader, in hot weather pitch your tent as far from your camels as you dare, and, if there be a breeze, to the windward!" [2]

Wayne quickly learned that, to avoid total chaos when his prize imported animals were taken from their quarters in Indianola, he had to send a rider ahead on horseback, shouting to teamsters, "Get out of the road; the camels are coming." This warning applied only to horses and mules; oxen paid the dromedaries no heed, continuing their steady pulling as the new animals passed close by.[3] Another problem with the camels in the vicinity of Indianola proved to be their willingness to eat anything. Many local citizens, unable to afford building a fence in the normal fashion, had planted rows of prickly pears to hold in their animals. Camels apparently found the cacti tasty, much to the anger of property owners. Fred Holzheuser recalled that his brother, when he caught camels eating his "fence," would ride out with his bull-whip and " 'cut-up' those camels severely with his whip. When he would whip them, they would outrun a horse." [4]

The camels, when they first landed, were in remarkably good health after their close confinement aboard ship, rapidly recovering their vigor. Some of the males, still in rutting season, proved "fierce and troublesome," as Wayne reported to Secretary of War Davis. But the major intended to have their packsaddles fitted soon to see "what effect a little gentle work . . . will have upon their tempers." Young boys in Indianola discovered that if they went to the place where the camels were watered, the male beasts would chase them about.

Within a week after landing, Wayne and wagonmaster Ray found they needed additional hay at the camel yard. The major, interested to learn more about public reaction to the animals, directed one of his men to take a camel to the Quartermaster forage house to get four bales. Wayne followed discreetly, mingling with the crowd that gathered in order to observe. The drover made the animal kneel and loaded two bales, totaling 613 pounds, whereupon some in the crowd expressed doubt that the camel could rise under such a burden. Then the drover packed two more bales on the beast, bringing the total weight of hay to 1256 pounds. By this time many of the spectators were stating openly that the animal could not rise, much less carry the weight. Wayne, who, of course, had been recognized, wrote of the moment, "I was regarded by some compassionate individuals as about to make a splendid failure." Yet at the drover's signal, the camel rose and walked away, much to the surprise of the assembled crowd. "It is sufficient to say that I was completely satisfied," Wayne wrote Davis. So impressed was one person in the crowd that he recorded this incident in verse, a poem subsequently published in the *Indianola Bulletin*.[5]

At this point, yet another of the camel's liabilities became obvious—its habit of emitting the most heart-rending and ear-splitting groans. When a dromedary is approached to be loaded or unloaded, it bleats out a harsh and ill-natured growl, especially if it feels it has been overloaded. Travelers visiting the desert have noted that a caravan, preparing for the day's march, can be heard for miles. Indeed, Father Huc wrote that once when a pack of wolves attacked, his drover put the pack to flight by "tweaking his camel's nose till he roared again."[6]

For almost three weeks Major Wayne kept the camels near Indianola, allowing the animals to recover somewhat from their recent voyage and practicing loading and unloading them. Small boys crowded eagerly around near the Quartermaster depot when they saw the beasts coming. The drovers, once at the yard, would use a switch to strike the animals gently on the legs, whereupon they would kneel. Wayne loaded them with sacks and boxes and small barrels and bales of hay—anything and everything to learn how various items fared when lashed to the saddle of a moving camel.

To his surprise the animals seemed little the worse for their

The method of riding a camel across the desert was totally different from anything in the American experience with horses and mules, as shown by this drawing which Henry C. Wayne submitted with his report to Jefferson Davis.

long confinement aboard ship. This, plus the impending advent of the rainy season on the coast of Texas, caused him to decide to move the animals farther inland. The rains, when they began, would turn Hog Wallow Prairie, as the forty miles of flat land near Indianola was called, into a quagmire impracticable for the beasts. Moreover, Wayne believed that "the air, water, and grass . . . would be better in the interior than so immediately upon the seaboard."

On the morning of June 4 the caravan set out, the camels loaded lightly. That first day's march proved difficult, for the road was bad, the animals "frisky and unruly," the new saddles kept slipping, and the loads needed constant readjustment. Nevertheless they covered twelve miles. The next day the road continued bad, and some of the weaker animals showed signs of fatigue; yet even with a two-hour rest at lunch, they marched for fifteen miles. The third day, June 6, Wayne led the caravan another five miles, whereupon he arrived at a beautiful prairie rich in grass. For five days he encamped to allow the camels to rest. Because this was only four and a half miles from the town of Victoria, many of the people living there went out in a carnival mood to see the strange animals.

Among these people was ten-year-old Pauline Shirkey. She went with her father, who fell into a conversation with Major Wayne. Pauline thought the major "one of the finest men I ever saw. He was handsome, and was very considerate of me." Actually Wayne was far more concerned about his camels than he was about most of the crowd; he did not want the people to get too near them for fear that the animals might be injured. Suddenly there occurred a camel wrestling match, although to young Pauline Shirkey it seemed that the two beasts were fighting. Months earlier Lieutenant Porter, in his long report to Secretary of War Davis, had penned a description of camel wrestling:

> Wrestling matches between camels [are] an amusement in which Turks take great delight, although they sometimes get a fine animal maimed in the sport. Many gentlemen keep them for no other purpose, and one person in Smyrna kept twenty at one time, for the amusement of his wife, who had a fondness for the sport. The

camels are trained to wrestling when quite young; they exhibit great dexterity in throwing their antagonists, and seem to take much pleasure in the fray. . . . When two strange [males] meet together where there are any females, they immediately have a wrestling match for the supremacy, and the conquered one ever afterwards acknowledges his inferiority by not so much as daring to look at a female. . . . Though the animals do sometimes get their legs broken, or are stiff for some time after with their bruises; well trained animals seldom injure each other, being taught to throw their antagonist by getting his neck under their fore leg (the right) and then throwing the whole weight of their body on him, and bringing him to the ground.

Porter had concluded that, because Americans loved both amusement and novelty, camel wrestling alone might endear the beast to his fellow countrymen "if their utility does not recommend them." [7]

Not only did Pauline Shirkey see a camel wrestling match, but she also observed yet another of the animal's liabilities, one that made many American handlers of the beast hate it. She recalled that when the animals became angry, they were able to blow something out of their insides, much like a balloon, bloody red in color, and dreadful in appearance. Major Wayne had noted this peculiarity in the report about camels he had written while crossing the ocean. During rutting season, he had stated, the camel's "excitement is often marked by a peculiar projection from his mouth of a loose, membranous lining of the throat, in the form and with the appearance of a bladder, accompanied by a loud, bubbling noise from the passage of the air with which it is inflated." [8]

While the herd was encamped near Victoria, Wayne came to the Shirkey house for dinner, during which he promised young Pauline that she could have a ride on one of the animals. Also, he presented to Pauline's mother, Mrs. Mary A. Shirkey, some of the hair which had been clipped from the camels. Of course, the hair smelled like camels. Mrs. Shirkey aired it out in the sun, after which she washed it again and again and even left it out at night for the dew to counteract the odor. Finally she carded the hair and spun it into thread, with which she knitted one sock. This she found far too coarse for the purpose she intended—a gift for President Franklin Pierce. Disappointed, Mrs. Shirkey spun yet finer thread and knitted a finer pair of socks. In the letter which accompanied this present to the President, she wrote, "If I had the machinery, I could have made you a better specimen of what the camel's wool could do in Texas." Several months later Mrs. Shirkey received a letter of thanks from the President, accompanied by a silver goblet inscribed with his name.[9]

True to his word, Wayne, when he started his caravan from the prairie outside Victoria toward San Antonio, gave Pauline Shirkey a ride on one of his prize animals. Although it seemed to the young girl that it was the middle of the day before the moment arrived, Wayne's report shows that the march began at 6:30 a.m. Wayne lifted her aboard a kneeling camel, and the ride began. "The camel-bells were jingling from the necks of the leaders," she recalled seventy-five years later, "and I was sitting high on the back of this unusual steed at whose head walked one of the Arabs, ever careful that no misfortune overcame me. After riding about two miles, we came to the nearest point to our home, and the caravan stopped and the camel kneeled. I descended and watched my friend Major Wayne, with his camels, leisurely proceed toward Victoria. I never saw them any more after that." [10]

That day the camels made eleven miles, the next seventeen and one-half, and on June 14 twenty-one miles. This was still not the distance Wayne hoped to make with fully loaded animals, but there was improvement. By June 16 they were at Cibolo where, almost a hundred years before, Spaniards had built a small fort to protect themselves from marauding Apaches and Comanches. By noon that day when the party camped, more than twelve miles had already been covered. However, at 1:30 that afternoon one of the females unexpectedly gave birth and the journey halted. The calf never held up its head, was breathing with difficulty, and died the next morning at 5:00 a.m. Wagonmaster Ray performed an autopsy and found the glands in the calf's throat were badly swollen, pressing in and closing its air passage, while its lungs were badly congested.

On June 17 the party had completed seventeen miles by 3:00 p.m., whereupon Wayne left Ray in charge and rode into San Antonio, a distance of twelve miles, to see what arrangements had been made for him by the local quartermaster. He found that an officer of that office had arranged for him to occupy a campground on the headwaters of the San Pedro River two miles from town; the land belonged to the city of San Antonio and had been made available free of charge. The following day, June 18, Ray brought the caravan to this area, which had good grass and water. Wayne, in making his report of the trip, noted that the roads had been hot and dusty and his camels only recently disembarked from long confinement aboard ship, but stated that they were in good condition. "After acclimation," he concluded, "I think they will be capable of rendering good service." [11]

Less than a week later, however, Wayne had moved his herd once again. He discovered, to his distress, that "proximity to town was not beneficial to my men or animals." The camel was capable of showing his true value only in transporting goods between centers of population; he was not an urban animal. Wayne therefore persuaded a nearby rancher to make land available on the Medina River twelve miles away from San Antonio, and by June 28 he reported to Davis that the transfer had been effected.

This raised in his mind the question of a permanent home for the camel. The geography in the vicinity of San Antonio he thought "well adapted to the acclimation and breeding of the camel," labor was cheap in that region and thus quarters for animals and men could be constructed inexpensively, and there was no danger from Indian raids. Yet he noted that the selection of permanent quarters for the camels raised a yet larger question: what were the views of the government as to the purpose of importing camels, and what uses were the animals to be put? He noted that the camel, on a comparative basis with other animals and with wagons, would prove of great utility and economy in transporting goods, and that it would be "a desirable addition to our stock of domestic animals." Then he asked, "Shall those, then, introduced be mainly devoted to breeding and increasing the number, or shall they be put to hard labor with the risk of being worn out in the service?"

Persuasively he tried to answer his own question to the satisfaction of his superiors so they would agree with him: "In my view, the introduction of the animal has been the primary object, and to achieve this will require time, five years at least." For proper testing of the animal, it should be given a permanent home where breeding experiments could be conducted, with labor restricted to transporting necessary supplies to that post. In this manner, he thought, "the race can be well spread through Texas" within ten years, and from there camels would spread to the rest of the nation. To use the few camels already imported strictly for military purposes would prove unwise, he believed, for the needs of the Army were too widespread and the number of camels too small. What was needed, he concluded, was for Jefferson Davis to make this decision in order to settle this broad philosophical question about the future of the Camel Corps.[12]

During this time Davis apparently was following events in the field closely. On July 5 he wrote directly to Wayne saying he had received news of the safe arrival of the camels in San Antonio in good condition, and he recommended that the animals be allowed to rest for some time before being put to work. "Horses, under the same circumstances," he noted, "would require many months to regain their full efficiency, and animals of a larger size would require a still longer period of rest." [13]

Yet when Jefferson Davis made his decision concerning the future of the Camel Corps, he did not send this directly to Wayne. Rather the bad news he sent to Quartermaster General Thomas S. Jesup in the form of an endorsement to Wayne's letter of June 28: "The establishment of a breeding farm did not enter into the plans of the department. The object at present is to ascertain whether the animal is adapted to the military service, and can be economically and usefully employed therein. When this is satisfactorily established, arrangements can be made for importing or breeding camels to any extent that may be deemed desirable." Jesup forwarded this terse statement without com-

Drawing of the use of camels as mobile artillery carriers. From Colnel F. Colombari's "The Zemboureks, or the Dromedary Field Artillery of the Persian Army."

ment, following it on July 30 with definite orders about housing the animals. Wayne was directed to locate them where they could demonstrate their fitness "for our military service." Until that was established, he said, "it is needless to inquire whether they may be bred in the United States." [14]

Ironically in this case the man in the field, Major Wayne, had taken a broader view of the long-range needs of the country and the Army than had the secretary of war in Washington. And the major had no choice but to obey orders. Davis' answer seemed to end forever any philosophical dispute about why camels had been imported, but the question would continue to arise—and the difference in viewpoint between the men working with the animals and those setting policy in the nation's capital would plague the experiment during the remainder of its life.

Wayne, meanwhile, was having some difficulty with the camels. On July 22 he reported that through neglect by his herders imported from the Middle East one of the female animals had strayed. A search was instituted, and the missing animal was found two miles away laying on its side and very ill. Under Ray's supervision it was returned to the ranch on the Medina, but died there a few hours later. A. Z. Herman, a medical doctor, was summoned and persuaded to perform an autopsy. This revealed that the animal had died as a result of "a heavy blow or blows inflicted on the neck of the animal, fracturing the clavicles in several places, and one dorsal and one side rib." Bone fragments had pierced the chest cavity, causing a severe inflammation of the lungs, which were filled with "bloody and frothy serum." Naturally the Arab herdsmen all denied any knowledge of what Wayne called "this brutal deed," and they testified to one another's innocence. Wayne wrote that this particular animal had been a gentle one so there was no possibility that the blows had been inflicted in self-defense.

This incident delayed his planned visit to Fort Martin Scott on a trip of inspection to see if this might be a suitable headquarters for the camels. This post had been established by the federal government in December of 1848 as part of an attempt to protect settlements in Texas from marauding Comanches. Situated on the banks of a branch of the Colorado River near the town of Fredericksburg, the fort was abandoned in 1852 and fell into private ownership. When Wayne visited there in 1856, the buildings were in disrepair because of neglect. There were no stables but there was an old storehouse capable of conversion to that use. Immediately around the dilapidated post consisted of "barren sand and post oak," offering little pasturage. Wayne noted that Fort Martin Scott was not a place "such as I would select," but would suffice if nothing better could be found. The owner, a civilian, offered to rent it to the government on a five- or ten-year lease for fifty dollars per month, along with grazing rights in the vicinity.

Wayne obviously had no desire to move to Fort Martin Scott. Rather he talked instead of visiting within the next week or two at Camp Verde, some sixty miles from San Antonio. Inasmuch as buildings for officers and men, along with stables already existed at that point, he thought it might be adapted to headquartering the camels with but a slight additional expense to the government. He concluded this report to Jefferson Davis by requesting, in a roundabout way, that the secretary of war re-examine his philosophy about the future of the Camel Corps, for he asked that he be "fully informed of your views in relation to the permanent disposition of the camels." Inasmuch as Quartermaster General Jesup had already communicated this information to him, Wayne definitely knew Davis' views; pretending ignorance, however, he asked for clarification—and, if possible, for Davis himself to answer directly so that no underling might distort them.[15]

A week later Wayne wrote to report the mysterious death of yet another camel. On the morning of August 4 the animal was found dead in its stall. Just the day before, he wrote, he had pointed this particular camel out to visitors as one of the most thriving in the herd, for she was "well and lively." No veterinarian available, he asked wagonmaster Ray to perform an autopsy on the dromedary, which was one of those given by the viceroy of Egypt as a present to the government of the United States; there was no external evidence of foul play, and Ray could find nothing internally wrong.[16]

Soon after this event Wayne set out to inspect Camp Verde, which he referred to as Green Valley, the English translation of its Spanish name, *Val Verde*. This post, located three miles from Bandera Pass on Verde Creek, had been established in July 1855. As he approached the post, Wayne noted an abundance of grass and water in the vicinity, lime to be had for burning plus sand and stone, and timber which could be converted to lumber and shingles; in short, building materials abounded in the vicinity. Wayne reported that with the aid of the soldiers at the post, plus civilian workers who could be hired cheaply, he could inexpensively erect all the buildings he might need.

In addition, the camels could be sent from Camp Verde to San Antonio and to other frontier posts to demonstrate their "adaptation to our climate, to the military service, and to commerce." In fact, he anticipated all types of experiments: freighting supplies, carrying express messages, and transporting infantrymen; and, he wrote, "one or more may be mounted with a small gun throwing shrapnell, &c." Apparently he had been impressed with the "gunships of the desert" which he had seen in the Middle East.

Wayne was pleased to find that Captain Innis N. Palmer, commander of the post, possessed "intelligence" and manifested an interest in the camel experiment. Both Wayne and Palmer had gone to West Point. Born in New York, Palmer had entered the Army in 1846 as a second lieutenant of mounted rifles after graduating from the Military Academy. For gallant and meritorious service at the Battle of Chapultepec in Mexico City in 1847, he had been breveted a first lieutenant, a rank to which he was promoted in 1853. On March 3, 1855, he transferred to the 2nd Cavalry as a captain and was sent to Texas where he assumed command at Camp Verde.[17] Wayne concluded from their conversations that Palmer would cooperate with the experiment "with judgment and zeal." He informed Secretary of War Davis that unless the mail brought him instructions to the contrary, he would commence preparations to move the camels to Camp Verde, and that after he arrived he would begin building stables for them.[18]

The move to Camp Verde was completed on August 26 and 27. Ray had charge of the camels and proceeded ahead of Wayne, who remained in San Antonio an extra day to hire workers to build the shelters he needed at the new home. He anticipated that these buildings would be completed within five or six weeks.[19] During these months Wayne's payroll had been increasing. In May, when the animals came ashore at Indianola, his payroll included:

Albert Ray, Clerk and Overseer,	$65 per month
Alexander Aslanyan, Interpreter	25 per month
Mahomet Meriwan, Camel Driver,	10 per month
Mahomet Iamar, Camel Driver	10 per month
Sylum Abu Agnam, Camel Driver	10 per month
Ali Oglou Suleiman, Camel Driver	10 per month
Mustafa Oglou Hassom, Camel Driver	10 per month
Total	$140 per month

The following month the payroll had increased by sixty dollars when Ali Oglou Suleiman and Mustafa Oglou Hassom had their pay increased to twenty dollars per month each, and John Swartz and John Ludwicke were hired at twenty dollars a month each as camel drivers.

July brought changes to the payroll. Mahomet Meriwan and Mahomet Iamar were fired "for causing death of camel," according to a notation on Wayne's payroll report, although no mention was made of this in his letters to Secretary of War Davis. John Swartz was discharged on July 31, his services no longer needed, while John Ludwicke was fired on July 13 for disobedience of orders. However, four new names appeared: Charles Hynes, Antonio Canales, Felix Polanco, and Macharias Baldez, all employed at twenty dollars a month, each listed as "Mexican Mule Packer."

August saw two new names on the payroll. Frederick William Feldstrop was employed at $52.40 per month as "Camel Master," and Francisco Morales became a "Mexican Mule Packer" at twenty dollars. Surprisingly, the two Arabian camel drivers supposedly discharged the previous month were still on the payroll and drawing their salaries, but Felix Polanco was listed as discharged as of August 31.

September's payroll still carried the clerk, camel master, and interpreter, along with the five Arabs imported to work with the animals, but mule packer Charles Hynes was discharged and Henry Floyd was hired in his place. While the expenses were remaining stable at approximately $200 per month, Wayne was spending $477.02 in August and September to employ a builder, masons, carpenters, and laborers to erect the stables he needed at Camp Verde. The builder received $150 per month for his services, masons were paid $50 per month, carpenters $50 per month or $1.50 per day, and ordinary laborers $20 per month.[20]

By the end of August, Wayne still had deposited to his account with Riggs & Company, bankers, of Washington the sum of $9920.77. This remained from the original $20,000 turned over to him when he departed for the Middle East to purchase the animals. On instructions from Secretary of War Davis, he transferred this amount to the assistant treasurer of the United States at New Orleans, placing it in an account entitled "appropriation for the purchase of camels." Thereafter he drew on this account to pay his bills.

By late September, Wayne could report that his camels were doing well, although one of the Bactrians and four of the animals from Smyrna seemed to be suffering from the heat. But he noted that the shelters for these animals, as well as those expected in December, were progressing rapidly toward completion. The camel corral at Camp Verde was an exact duplicate of the *khan* of the Middle East; almost rectangular, it had walls ten feet high and each 150 feet long. These walls were of lumber with stone and adobe laid over. Immediately behind the corral, the five native camel drovers erected huts adjoining the rear wall.

The construction nearing completion, Wayne found time to talk to civilian ranchers in the vicinity to learn their experiences in importing animals. He was told that no animals, brought full grown into Texas, were as vigorous in their new home as in their old, "the process of acclimation impairing, apparently, vital energy and endurance." However, offspring of such animals, he was told, were the reverse: more energetic than their parents had ever been. If such proved to be the case, he noted, slyly injecting a thought about the philosophy which should guide the Camel Corps for the future, "we must look to the produce of the present importations." Meanwhile, he believed that the experiment should continue, remembering that the animals in use were not a true test of the dromedary's ability for the stock was "deteriorated."

And Major Wayne was experimenting with the animals. On August 28 three wagons from Camp Verde set out for San Antonio to bring oats to the post. Ray was sent with six camels to accompany the wagons. Wayne reported that the sixty-mile trip to town took three days because the wagons, although empty, were slowed because the mules pulling them suffered from want of water. The camels, he noted, could have made the journey in two days. In San Antonio on Monday, September 1, the camels were loaded with 3648 pounds of oats, an average of 608 pounds each, and departed at noon, arriving at Camp Verde at 6:00 p.m. on Wednesday, September 3. Wayne wrote that they had traveled leisurely and with less weight than they were capable of carrying. The wagons, meanwhile, left San Antonio on Tuesday at noon

A prize riding camel from the Mount Sinai area. Drawing by Gwinn Harris Heap.

and reached Camp Verde at 12:30 p.m. on Saturday; although each wagon was pulled by a six-mule team and had a total cargo of approximately 3700 pounds of oats, the camels made the same trip in forty-two and one-half hours less time.

Wayne cautioned this one experiment did not prove that six camels were superior to twelve mules and two good wagons. "But I mean to say that, viewed in relation to this vast unsettled country, where the roughness of roads limits materially the loads placed in the wagons, and where the general want of water throughout regulates the day's journey of mules, six camels will accomplish as much as two six-mule teams, and in less time, and at much less expense." Nor had the camels gone directly overland to San Antonio, which would have saved several miles, because the land was too rough for the wagons.

On September 8 Wayne had an opportunity to test the capabilities of a camel on a rough, overland trip without roads. Because Indians had been observed in the vicinity—perhaps coming to see the new and strange animals about which so many people were talking—a lieutenant of cavalry and a small detachment of troops were sent in pursuit. Wayne suggested that a dromedary accompany the party to carry provisions for the seven men and corn for their equal number of horses. The following day the lieutenant returned to report that the dromedary followed the horses wherever they went, "not only keeping up with them, but showing that, if not restrained, he would have gone ahead of them." This with a load of 300 to 400 pounds.

When soldiers at this small post expressed an interest in the experiment, Wayne allowed them to be instructed in the mysteries of packing and managing his camels. Because of the hump on the animal just brought to Texas, packing was different from the previous experience the soldiers had had with mules. The pack saddle of the camel, so these soldiers learned, consisted of three parts: a cylindrical pad, a wooden frame, and a girth. The pad, of loosely woven wool or camelhair cloth, generally was stuffed with straw and was fitted over the hump. Then came the frame, made of two cross bars of hard wood shaped in the form of the letter V but reversed and joined near the top by two horizontal transverse

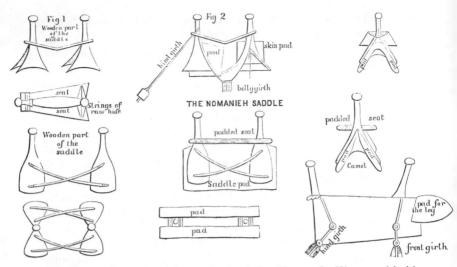

Drawings of camel saddles, submitted by Henry C. Wayne with his report to Secretary of War Jefferson Davis; the drawing is from Colonel F. Colombari's "The Zemboureks, or the Dromedary Field Artillery of the Persian Army."

pieces of wood; when placed on the camel, one of the crossbars went in front of the hump, the other behind it. Once on the animal, this frame was fastened by two girths, one in front and the other in back; the girth, passing around the animal at its most sensitive point, was generally covered with sheepskin with the wool still on and had to be cleaned frequently. Moreover, the lashing ropes for the cargo had to be of a soft texture, for the animal's skin was easily chafed.

During the saddling, a camel had to be made to kneel for the pad and frame to be put on, then made to stand while the girth was being fastened, then made to kneel again to be loaded. During this time the animal made a medley of loud noises: growling, groaning, snoring, bleating, snarling, and wheezing—and, on most occasions when it had a sufficiency of water, spat indiscriminately at the men around it. This proved to be yet another of the camel's liabilities not mentioned by those who had wanted to import it. A ruminant like the cow, the camel's food when first swallowed passed to its first stomach. After the hay, oats, or whatever it had eaten was partially digested in that stomach, the animal then regurgitated it into its mouth for further chewing—or spitting. The cud was a foul-smelling, sticky mass which the soldiers told one another would cause terrible sores.

The soldiers were not noted for their kindness to their horses or mules, and to them the camel seemed a beast straight from Satan's own herd. It had an odor that would sober a drunk man; it groaned and bleated in noisy fashion; it spat without provocation; it loaded in a different fashion from "civilized" animals; and in the spring when it began to shed its winter coat of hair, it looked as if it was harboring the most dreaded skin disease. Yet woe to the soldier who, in frustration, tried to beat the animal "to get its attention," as these men said when they struck a mule.

At Camp Verde just after the camels first arrived, one soldier learned the hard way that these animals could defend themselves. A private detailed to practice loading and unloading the animal, he piled too much on to suit the beast and it began to groan and make known its unhappiness in the usual camel fashion. The soldier decided to show the animal who was boss, as he might have a mule, by kicking it sharply in the belly, whereupon the camel turned and spat a wad of its foul-smelling cud into his face. Enraged, the soldier grabbed a club and swung at the dromedary's head. The dromedary dodged the blow easily, gave forth a shrill scream, and in one quick motion ripped the man's arm to the bone with its sharp incisors.

Actually the soldier was lucky—although no doubt he did not consider himself so—for the camel could just as easily have used its canine teeth and incisors to bite off his arm or his kneecap. Moreover, a camel always remembered those who mistreated him and would wait to even the score; "the 'camel's temper' is a proverbial expression used by the Arabs to denote a vindictive and unforgiving disposition," George P. Marsh had written. When once thoroughly angered at someone, the animal would wait for a chance; then, if possible, he would knock the person down and lay on him, crushing the enemy with his great weight.[21]

Major Wayne, who gave orders to these men and was not directly involved, was not fully aware of the hatred that was developing for the camel. Instead, he continued his experiments, writing happily to Jefferson Davis after each. One of these began on October 1. That day twelve camels set out for San Antonio under the direction of Albert Ray, the clerk and overseer. Ray was instructed to take the regular road both going and coming back. However, on the trip to San Antonio, Ray claimed to have lost the road because of its indistinctness, and turned aside; after going ten miles, he discovered his error and returned to the right road. Still he reached San Antonio "easily in two days" after a trip of eighty miles. The next two days, Saturday and Sunday, it rained at San Antonio, wetting the roads and making them muddy and boggy. Under these conditions wagons normally did not travel, for the soil in that area became gummy when wet and would stick firmly to the wheels; each time the wheel turned, it picked up yet another layer until it was encased in a thick sheath of soil that made travel progressively slower and more laborious for the animals.

Ray decided that these conditions offered another opportunity for testing the camel. He had been with Wayne and Lieutenant Porter on the trip to the Middle East and was familiar with the literature they had gathered. Among this information was a report on the uses of the camel by General J. L. Carbuccia of the French Army, who had written that on muddy roads "the camel falls upon his knees, his fore feet slipping. He does not then try to rise but goes on in that position, nor does he try to right himself until he is out of the bad part of the road. He easily slips on clay soil, especially after rain. He should in such case be brought to a halt, as he is liable to break his legs, especially the hinder ones." [22]

Loading each animal with an average of 325 pounds, Ray and his camel drovers set out at noon on October 5 when there was a temporary halt in the rain. However, the moisture quickly returned, coming down in torrents on Monday and Tuesday. Nevertheless, the caravan reached Camp Verde on Tuesday evening, October 7, and delivered 3800 pounds of oats. Wayne noted that "experienced disinterested persons said at the time that loaded

An "arvana camel" from Asia Minor, as drawn by Gwinn Harris Heap.

wagons could not have traveled in such weather," but that the rain had slowed the camels but little. He concluded this report by stating that all the animals were in good health except for three: a Bactrian that was teething and two dromedaries that had been severely bitten by other animals.[23]

Two weeks later Wayne wrote the secretary of war to report that the Bactrian, along with one of the camels that had been bitten, had died. Enclosed with this letter was one written by Albert Ray, who had been commissioned to conduct an autopsy. He wrote that the Bactrian, which had been named Gusuf, had seemed in good health, but that he had found the liver to be totally diseased; although the animal had been dead only a few hours, the liver was "putrescent and offensive," filled with cysts and pus. He concluded that apparently the disease was "of long standing, and being aggravated by confinement on shipboard, change of food and climate, at last resulted in the death of the camel."

The other animal, in his opinion, had died of external wounds. On the previous October 5 it had been grazing in a pasture when it was attacked by Mahomet, the animal presented by the bey of Tunis; with its teeth, Mahomet had inflicted a severe, deep cut on the inside of the left thigh of the Egyptian camel. The wound had been carefully treated but had proved so sore that the Egyptian animal was unable to walk, kneel down, or graze, and on November 17 it finally died. In trying to perform the autopsy, Ray had made an incision in the vicinity of the wound, and out poured more than half a gallon of pus.[24]

The elections of November 1856, wherein James Buchanan had been elected president, meant that a shakeup of the cabinet likely would follow. Major Wayne realized that Jefferson Davis likely would not continue as secretary of war, and therefore he wrote on December 4 to get his recommendations on record for whoever succeeded to that office. In addition, he found his own position increasingly difficult, and for that reason he wanted to be relieved of his responsibility with the camels. Captain Palmer, the commander at Camp Verde, had cooperated in every way possible, but Wayne found other line (cavalry) officers prejudiced against him because he, a staff officer, was senior to them; the result was that he had little control over the enlisted men at the post. "I have no desire to hold a questionable position," he wrote, although his request for a transfer was contrary to his personal wishes.

In this letter he recommended that the camels be placed under the authority of an "intelligent regimental captain" who would take an interest in them and who shared the same vision as Wayne that the animals should receive a fair test. No civilian should be placed in charge of the camels. Also, he thought that the climate and topography in the vicinity of Camp Verde were ideal, and that the animals should not be moved from the region. At that post the beasts were well sheltered, and everything had been prepared for the rutting season, which was about to commence. His recommendation was that Captain Palmer could handle the chore provided Albert Ray was continued with the project; Ray was experienced with the animals and possessed veterinary skills.

One last time Wayne strove to have his philosophical views about the future of the project prevail: "The experiment to be fairly determined will require time, five or six years at least." He concluded that the camel already had proved its military useful-ness and that it could adapt to the climate of Texas.[25]

Jefferson Davis, eager to see Major Wayne and to receive in person his report about the camels, replied on December 13 that Wayne was to journey to Washington and then was to proceed to New Orleans to meet Lieutenant Porter and the *Supply*, due to ar-rive at the Crescent City about January 20, 1857, with the second load of camels.[26] Wayne was unable to comply immediately, however, for he was in Indianola to attend a military inquest. That did not end until January 10, after which Wayne returned to Camp Verde to pay his workers for December. There he learned that during his absence the remaining Bactrian camel had died of what he thought to be "the acclimatory disease of Texas, known as the 'Spanish fever.' " He noted that only the Bactrians had shown any ill effects from the climate. In all, five animals of the original thirty-four had died: the two Bactrians, two by vio-lent injuries, and one "by epilepsy, a disease to which the camel is said to be peculiarly liable." He had been able to detect no difference in the condition of the dromedaries from Egypt and the burden camels of Asia Minor; all seemed to find the climate of Texas equally agreeable. He concluded that fewer camels had died than would have been the case with horses or mules similarly imported.

His business at Camp Verde completed, Wayne took his final leave of the camels on January 19 and began the long journey to Washington to report to Secretary of War Davis. At Indianola he asked Captain Van Bokkelen to arrange for the care of the second load of camels, expected shortly, and at New Orleans he left Albert Ray, who was to accept the new cargo of camels from Lieutenant Porter and conduct them to Texas.

In Washington he conferred with Davis and then, at the orders of the secretary of war, he drafted his recommendations for the future of the Camel Corps. In his introductory paragraph Wayne commented that from 1848, when he first became interested in dromedaries, to 1857, he had never regarded the importation of camels as something of immediate benefit; rather he saw the experiment as "a legacy to posterity, of precisely the same character as the introduction of the horse and other domestic animals by the early settlers of America." Thus while carrying out the mandate of Congress to test the camel for military purposes, the major goal should be breeding and spreading the animals across the continent. He believed that it had been demonstrated that the camel could be successfully imported and acclimatized. "The breeding and the character of the stock yet remain to be shown; and for this time and careful management are required." What the military might do with camels was but of little moment when compared with benefits to be derived for business and transportation if the experiment was continued by far-sighted men.

Therefore he recommended that the animals imported should have a fixed home for three or four years. There they should be carefully tended while short experiments in transportation and scouting were conducted. Inasmuch as Camp Verde offered ideal conditions, he thought the herd should be kept there. Twenty or twenty-five enlisted men, including three or four non-commissioned officers, should be assigned to the Camel Corps while the

A female camel suckling her calf. Drawing by Gwinn Harris Heap.

officer in command of the project should be someone of "judgment and discretion." And this officer should "have as few military superiors over him as may be consistent with the laws and rules of service, both as a matter of justice to his individual reputation, and for the stronger reason that with a division of control and accountability responsibility ceases." [27]

While Wayne was in Washington drafting these recommendations—which amounted to a restatement of the philosophy he had expressed time and again, and which he hoped would shape the experiment in the future—he received word from Joseph R. Smith, an assistant surgeon at Camp Verde, that the camels were in fine condition despite the cold weather that winter. He noted that another calf had been stillborn, as had all the calves born since the original herd arrived in Texas. Surgeon Smith concluded that "most, if not every one, of the camels begotten on ship-board will be still-born." The reason to him was obvious: "the unusual and unnatural sea voyage." Captain I. N. Palmer, who also wrote Wayne of this stillborn calf, stated that Alexander Aslanyan, the interpreter, attributed the death to the mother having been "hurt or frightened." Palmer noted that almost all the females were pregnant and seemed to be "doing very well." [28]

Wayne thus terminated his duties with the Camel Corps just as the second shipment was arriving at New Orleans. Lieutenant Porter and Gwinn Harris Heap likewise concluded their work, leaving the camels in Texas temporarily in the charge of Captain Innis N. Palmer and clerk Albert Ray. Jefferson Davis was to be relieved as secretary of war after the change of administrations in March of 1857; James Buchanan would install a new secretary of war, one whose views would shape the future of the project, not the recommendations of Wayne or Porter or Heap or even Jefferson Davis. For his work in this experiment, Wayne later received a gold medal from the Société Imperial Zoologique de'Acclimation de Paris, but could only watch while another carried out the first major trek across the continent with camels.

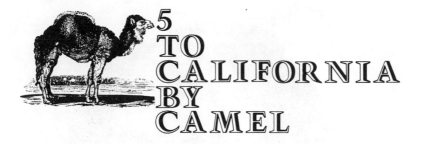

5
TO CALIFORNIA BY CAMEL

Secretary of War John B. Floyd proved as sympathetic to the Camel Corps and its use in the Southwest as had Jefferson Davis—and even more determined to use the dromedaries for military purposes alone. Born on June 1, 1806, in Montgomery County, Virginia, the son of a governor of that state, he grew to manhood on the frontier a vigorous young athlete. He was educated largely by his mother and by reading in his father's excellent library, graduating in 1829 from South Carolina College. After his marriage in 1830, he was caught up in the Arkansas cotton boom and moved to that state to practice law and raise cotton. When the Panic of 1837 hit, however, he lost both his fortune and his health, a fever leaving him weak for years.

Returning to Virginia, he practiced law at Abingdon so successfully that he was able to pay off his debts and rise socially again. In 1847 he was elected to the General Assembly and then re-elected the following year; in that assembly he advocated internal improvements with state subsidies, especially the building of railroads. Then in 1849 he was elected to a three-year term as

Secretary of War John B. Floyd. *Courtesy U. S. Signal Corps (Brady Collection, National Archives.*

governor and worked to improve conditions in the western part of the state as well as to bring industry to Virginia. A staunch states' rights Democrat, he was a presidential elector in that party in 1852 and fought hard against the Know-Nothing Party in 1855. On October 2, 1856, he was asked to give a speech in support of Democratic candidate James Buchanan at the Merchant's Exchange in New York City, and did this so ably that Buchanan appointed him secretary of war in the cabinet taking the oath of office in March of 1857.[1]

A subject of wide interest in Washington that spring was the building of wagon roads to California, a task that fell to the Army—and thus was under the direction of the secretary of war. Floyd, long an advocate of internal improvements, approved these roads, and he quickly displayed an interest in the Camel Corps. Why not join the two? Congress on February 14, 1857, had passed a bill authorizing construction of a federal road from El Paso to Fort Yuma, and it appropriated $200,000 for the project. Three days later, outgoing President Franklin Pierce had signed it.[2] Secretary of War Floyd conceived the surveying of a federal wagon road across the 35th parallel from Fort Defiance, New Mexico, to the Colorado River. The purpose of this road would be to move supplies overland from the Colorado to military posts in Arizona and New Mexico, for in 1857 the War Department already had put in motion a plan to send a steamboat up the Colorado to test its navigability above Fort Yuma. A wagon road from the Colorado across to New Mexico was the next logical step, and to secure the funds from Congress a survey would have to be made.

As Floyd searched about for the proper leader for this expedition with the camels, his attention was drawn to the name Edward Fitzgerald Beale. A man who once had traveled across the continent with Kit Carson, carrying in his saddlebags a copy of the recently published *Travels in Tartary, Thibet, and China*, by Abbe Huc, in order to read aloud from it by firelight in the evenings, Beale found himself early in 1857 in Washington defending his reputation. He had been appointed Superintendent of Indian Affairs for California in 1852, and under his direction large sums of money had been spent. Late in 1856 a political enemy in California, Joel H. Brooks, implied to certain congressmen that Beale had in his possession $351,666.98 of government funds, for which he had not been held accountable. On February 20, 1857, the Senate passed a resolution asking for all correspondence between the Treasury and Interior departments and Beale, along with all accounts and remittances. A study of these documents revealed that Beale had in his possession only $3723.97, which he immediately delivered to the Treasury Department; all other funds had been expended legally and correctly. The second comptroller, J. M. Brodhead, concluded, "As to Joel H. Brooks, the evidence shows him to be a worthless vagabond, whose testimony ought not to taint for a moment the character of any man having pretensions to a decent position before the world." [3]

Exonerated, Beale went to his hometown of Chester, Pennsylvania, to visit, and there he was contacted by Secretary of War Floyd about taking charge of the Camel Corps to survey a wagon road from Fort Defiance, New Mexico, across the 35th parallel to the Colorado River. Despite the fact that this trek would be made during the coming summer when water and forage would be scarce and the heat intense, Beale replied with an enthusiastic acceptance. Naturally this proposed expedition excited the townspeople of Chester, for both Lieutenant David D. Porter and Gwinn Harris Heap were natives. Immediately many young men of the town expressed an interest in seeing the desert Southwest by accompanying Beale, and three of them succeeded: Hampden Porter, son of Dr. James Porter; Porter Heap, son of Gwinn Harris Heap; and May Humphreys Stacey, son of Davis Bevan Stacey. They were made assistants, and as such would accompany the survey.

The three adventuresome young men arrived in Philadelphia on May 12 and that same day departed by train for Pittsburgh, there to meet Beale three days later. From there they continued by train to Cincinnati, where they boarded a steamboat that took them to New Orleans on May 26. They completed their purchase of supplies and on June 2, in the midst of torrential rains, boarded yet another steamer for the voyage to Indianola on the coast of

Texas. Four days later they were ashore at their destination. Harnessing their mules to the wagons they had brought, they then set out for San Antonio. Nineteen-year-old May Humphreys Stacey, who kept a detailed journal of this trip, wrote that the prairie affected him deeply: "A feeling of insignificance and worthlessness I felt when I gazed over the wide expanse of land—and my eyes were opened to the magnificence of Almighty God." [4]

By June 13 both men and animals were tired, for Beale was pushing them hard to reach Camp Verde as soon as possible. The wind was from the south, hot, sultry, and dry. That morning Porter Heap was placed in charge of the wagon train. Eighteen miles later they came to a valley through which flowed a stream; the first eight wagons got through safely, and Heap, thinking all would make it easily, continued with the lead wagon. However, two wagons failed to get through until much later that day, and then only after great labor. When they arrived in camp, Beale was with them—and in a bad humor.

A geologist said to him, "Mr. Beale, you look tired." He replied angrily, "I am not tired, but most damnably disgusted," and he confronted young Heap, telling him that he had not performed his duties as wagonmaster. Heap protested that he had not come on the expedition to be wagonmaster, but Beale continued to berate and belittle him. Finally Heap was moved to respond with anger, "Sir, I will not submit to this. I resign my post tomorrow."

Stacey was horrified that the party was to lose "a gentleman, a man of honor, and a friend." He thought it boded ill for the future, for he confided to his journal that evening, "Everything seems to be going wrong, and it is my opinion, founded on the remarks of others, that the party will never get through." Stacey little realized that the West was different from Chester, Pennsylvania, and that a leader such as Beale had to demand responsibility from everyone.

When they arrived in San Antonio on June 16, they encamped in a barnyard "covered with manure," and it proved to be "tenanted by fleas, in such marvelous quantities as to prevent a weary traveler from seeking the natural rest which God intended him to have. The little monsters penetrate into the folds of your woolen shirt, and remain quiet until you attempt to go to sleep, when they bring their batteries to bear, and woe be unto him who has not a thick hide."

Beale had decided to push ahead to Camp Verde in order to bring the camels to San Antonio to be loaded. There he learned what had transpired since Wayne's departure from the little post. The forty-one camels taken ashore at Indianola on February 10 from the *Suwanee* had been stabled at the same camel yard as before. Captain W. K. Van Bokkelen of the Quartermaster Corps had found it necessary to rent an additional warehouse at twenty dollars a month to store hay for the beasts while they rested after their long voyage.[5] There on March 3 in a row at a local saloon, William Kaufman, one of the men hired by Lieutenant Porter in Smyrna the previous November to care for this load of camels, was mortally wounded. He died the following day.[6]

By mid-April all of the new animals had recovered sufficiently to be sent on to Camp Verde, and on April 24 Captain R. E. Clay of the Quartermaster's Office at Indianola requested guidance about the ground that had been leased for their "accommodation."

This grizzled male Bactrian, as drawn by Gwinn Harris Heap, was from central Asia; note the long mane.

The question at hand really was whether or not additional camels would be imported by the Army. If the answer was negative, Clay needed an order to end the lease and dispose of the sheds that had been erected there at the expense of the government—an estimate of the total cost rendered by Captain Van Bokkelen showed that $1752 of Army funds had been used to purchase the lumber, shingles, nails, and cedar posts used to build them. On May 19 Clay was told to dispose of the sheds for what he could get for them and to end the lease on the plot of ground where the animals had been stabled.[7]

In this same correspondence was a notation "that the men at Camp Verde have not been paid." With Major Henry C. Wayne gone, apparently for good, Captain Innis N. Palmer had received no orders authorizing him to draw funds from the camel account even to pay salaries. On May 20 he had written to his superiors on this score, but no answer returned until much later, in August.

On June 19 Beale left Camp Verde with twenty-five camels, the best of the lot. Left behind at the post were forty-six camels, thirty-four adults and twelve calves. The twenty-five selected to make the journey across the 35th parallel were driven to San Antonio, arriving there on June 21. May Humphreys Stacey recorded the scene when the animals arrived at his flea-, fly-, and mosquito-infested camp:

> The first intimation we had of their approach was the jingling of the large bells suspended from their necks. Presently, one, then two, three, four, until the whole twenty-five had come within range in the dim twilight. And thus they came, these huge ungainly beasts of the desert, accompanied by their attendants, Turks, Greeks and Armenians. . . . Our mules and horses were very much frightened at the approach of the camels. They dashed around the corral, with heads erect and snorting in wild alarm. However, in a few hours they became more quiet.

Growing philosophical at this scene, Stacey wondered, "What are these camels the representation of? Not a high civilization exactly, but of the 'go-aheadness' of the American character, which subdues even nature by its energy and perseverance."

The next three days were spent in feverish activity; loading wagons, arranging packs, seeing to last minute details, and readying for the march to begin. Unfortunately during these three days, an extremely serious problem arose—the "Turks" hired by Wayne and Porter refused to accompany the expedition. The men were unhappy because they had not been paid according to the contract they had signed with the government of the United States; since January, when Wayne last paid them, they had received nothing, although, noted Beale, they had "performed their duties very faithfully." Inasmuch as the civilians with Beale little understood how to pack camels, the beginning of the march was slowed that first day, June 25, 1857.[8] Beale reluctantly placed the animals in the care of A. Breckenridge, Jr., with I. D. Morley and James Via to assist him.

The first day the expedition made only sixteen miles. Beale noted that the camels had grown lazy from their easy living at Camp Verde, but he expressed hope that they soon would become hardened by the trail. And half-wild mules caused difficulties. Young Stacey, observing the camels that first day, concluded that "these camels will prove a failure," for he thought in the Middle East they had carried only fruits, wine, and other local products of little weight; because the animals on this expedition were carrying an average of 576 pounds, he thought they would "fail to make any reasonable speed."

On the second day's march, Stacey's pessimism seemed justified, for two of the camels became ill. Their loads were placed on wagons, and they were allowed to accompany the expedition unencumbered (later they became well and resumed working). By the end of the fourth day, Beale reported that the dromedaries were browsing on mesquite bushes "and the leaves of a thorny shrub, which grows in this country everywhere." Also, he commented that the animals were "exceedingly docile, easily managed, and I see, so far, no reason to doubt the success of the experiment."

On June 30 they arrived at Fort Clarke (near the present Bracketville, Texas), after which they entered a country of less rainfall—and consequently of a more barren appearance. However, to Stacey this was the beginning of adventure: "Here we can consider ourselves fairly in the Indian Country, dependent upon ourselves alone for protection from the unrelenting hands of merciless savages." The streams and creeks along the road toward Fort Davis proved to be especially low that year, but Beale happily could report the camels were hardening; on July 2 he wrote, "The camels . . . arrived shortly after the wagons. I am much encouraged to see how eagerly they seek the bushes for food instead of grass, which certainly indicates their ability to subsist much easier than horses and mules in countries where forage is scarce."

July 4 proved to be rainy and miserable. On the trail wagons became mired in mud and had to be pulled out with ropes, men issuing forth "more cursing, and strange oaths" than under ordinary circumstances. But the camels plodded along patiently and "stood the storm better than I thought they would," wrote Beale. Soon the days began to blend one into another, each exactly the same. For several days after July 4 rain continued to fall, making men, horses, and mules miserable. Only the camel seemed to take no note, giving voice in the morning to his reluctance to be loaded but then bearing the burden quietly until the evening. On July 5 Beale noted in his journal of the expedition that they had encountered the eastern limit of a shrub that would be found for the remainder of their trip, a plant known by Westerners as greasewood. "I was delighted to see the camels eagerly seek it," wrote Beale, "and eat it with the greatest apparent relish. It is certainly very gratifying to find these animals eating, by their own preference, the coarse and bitter herbs, hitherto of no value, which abound always in the most sterile and desolate parts of every road." Horses and mules disdained greasewood, but camels ate it eagerly.

By July 8 Beale was becoming extremely interested in this strange animal bearing so much of his supplies. The greatest difficulty with them, he noted, was that he had no one who knew how to pack them. In consequence, many of the animals had sores on their backs where their packs rubbed them. However,

Gwinn Harris Heap's drawing of a Bactrian camel from the Crimea.

Beale commented that the animals seemed to heal much more rapidly than horses or mules; when a camel was found with a sore, it was relieved of its pack for a day or two and then was ready to work again. Also, he wrote that the dromedaries seemed "indifferent to the best grass," preferring "herbs and boughs of bitter bushes, which all other animals reject." He concluded, "Their perfect docility and patience under difficulties render them invaluable, and my only regret at present is that I have not double the number." By this time the loaded camels were arriving each evening at camp at the same time as the wagons.

Beale had crossed the continent several times and knew the dangers of the country they were traversing. The Comanches were the true masters of West Texas in 1857, although the Army maintained a chain of forts in the area in a futile attempt to halt Indian raids. The expedition was following what was known as the Lower Road, which ran from San Antonio to El Paso (the other road between these two cities was called, naturally, the Upper Road). Almost every mile of this road had seen some pilgrim or another killed, and graves abounded along it where victims of Comanche wrath had been buried. Beale did not laugh at the imagination of his men, which made them see Indians where none existed; rather he used this to advantage, writing on July 8: "This evening many of our party have seen Indians, but for me, 'Ah! sinner that I am, I was not permitted to witness so glorious a sight.' I encouraged the young men, however, in the belief that deer, bushes, &c., which they have mistaken for Indians, are all veritable Comanches, as it makes them watchful on guard at night."

By July 11 the camels had shown their true worth on the trail, and Beale was writing openly of his admiration of them:

> The camels are now keeping up easily with the train, and came into camp with the wagons. My fears as to their feet giving out, as I had been led to believe from those who seemed to know, have so far proved entirely unfounded, though the character of the road is exceedingly trying to brutes of any kind. My dogs cannot travel at all upon it, and after going a short distance run to the wagons and beg to be taken in. The camels, on the contrary, have not evinced the slightest distress or soreness; and this is the more remarkable as mules or horses, in a very short time, get so sore-footed that shoes are indispensable. The road is very hard and firm, and strewn all over it is a fine, sharp, angular, glinty gravel.

He concluded that the camels could "travel continuously in a country where no other barefooted beast could last a week." On July 16 he noted that these animals would "live on anything, and thrive. Yesterday they drank water for the first time in twenty-six hours, and although the day had been excessively hot they seemed to care but little for it." Mules, he noted, would under similar circumstances have been wild and nearly useless, if not broken down.

Arriving safely at Fort Davis, where repairs were made on wagons, the expedition continued westward. As the amount of supplies to be carried by the camels dwindled, Beale had their packs removed to allow their backs to recover from the sores that had rubbed on them. His conclusion was that they had suffered less than other pack animals would have, but was convinced they would do even better with "a better and lighter saddle." He noted that he intended to submit ideas on that score.

Arriving at the little village of San Elizario, just downriver from El Paso, the expedition was met by almost the entire Mexican population eager for a glance at the strange animals. Stacey commented that "plenty of Greasers, anxious to get a sight of the great wonder, the camel," came out, followed them through town, and out to the place where they camped for the night. At Fort Bliss on July 27 they drew supplies and proceeded up the Rio Grande toward Fort Fillmore and the town of Mesilla (present-day Las Cruces, New Mexico)—and there they encountered "screw-beans . . . [which] the camels seem to like . . . better than any other we have met with. Although the branches are covered with sharp thorns, larger and stronger than those which grow on the rose bush, the camel seizes them in his mouth and draws the limb through his teeth, rapidly stripping off the leaves and briars and eating both greedily."

At El Paso, Beale was surprised to be joined by some of the "Greeks and Turks" who at San Antonio had refused to make the trip. Apparently they had changed their minds and hurried after the caravan. However, Beale was sorely disappointed in them, writing to Secretary of War Floyd on July 24 that the newcomers "know no more of camels than any American living in New York knows of buffalo." He noted that he employed them anyway because his own men assumed these camel drovers knew everything about camels and thereby gained confidence in the face of an animal "which, with all its gentleness, has a most ferocious looking set of teeth which it displays with a roar rivaling that of the royal Bengal tiger." [9]

Proceeding up the Rio Grande, the caravan passed through many small Mexican villages, and at each the population crowded out to see the camels. Beale included in his journal the conversation he had at one such village with "a slouchy looking ruffian" who acted as spokesman for the local citizens. Looking at Beale's wagon, which "the taste of the builder had painted a bright red," the Mexican asked, "Dis show wagon, no?"

Rather than argue, Beale replied, "Yes."

"Ah, ha! You be dee showmans, no?"

"Yes, sir."

"What you gottee more on camelos? Gottee any dogs?" the Mexican wanted to know.

Beale did not disappoint him. "Yes, monkeys too, and more."

"Whattee more?"

"Horses more."

"Whattee can do horse?"

"Stand on his head, and drink a glass of wine."

The Mexican was impressed. "Valgame Dios!" he exclaimed. "What a people these are to have a horse stand on his head, and drink a glass of wine."

At last the caravan arrived in Albuquerque, encamping some two miles out while Beale rode on to Santa Fe to report to the commanding officer for the military district; there he arranged for additional supplies and worked out the details of a military escort for his caravan. That concluded, he returned to Albuquerque on August 12 to find that some of his men had succumbed to temptation of the flesh in that town. "This morning," he wrote dryly, "I was obliged to administer a copious supply of the oil of boot to several, especially to my Turks and Greeks. . . . The former had not found, even in the positive prohibitions of the prophet a sufficient reason for temperance, but was as drunk as any Christian in the train, and would have remained behind, but for a style of reason much resorted to by the head of his church, as well as others, in making converts, *i.e.*, a broken head." Billy Consodine, one of the Americans in Beale's camp, remarked that a cut-glass decanter well thrown was a prime mover for such people, but Beale disagreed: ". . . To move a stubborn half-drunken Turk give me a good tough piece of wagon spoke, aimed tolerably *high*." The Turk was Hadji Ali, whom the Americans commonly referred to as Hi-Jolly.

Leaving Albuquerque on August 13, the caravan traveled westward slowly, for Beale was awaiting the arrival of men bound for Fort Defiance under command of Colonel Loring. Each camel was loaded according to his size and strength, the largest with 1000 pounds on his back; the average weight was 700 pounds apiece. On August 20, after pushing slowly westward, Beale grew impatient at waiting for Loring and mounted a large white camel stallion named Seid. Traveling at the rate of eight miles an hour for thirteen and one-half miles, he found Loring; then, "finding his animals unequal to mine, I rode on to camp alone, and arrived after an absence of three hours, during which I had ridden twenty-seven miles." Seid was not noticeably tired, although he had worked hard the previous day. "The best horse or mule in our camp," Beale commented by way of comparison, "could not have performed the same journey in twice the time, although they have been fed with corn ever since leaving. . . ."

On August 24 Beale sent his caravan westward along the 35th parallel while he detoured to Fort Defiance. At last the expedition had reached the point where its real work could commence—a survey of a wagon road westward to the Colorado River. Beale was aware of the heavy responsibility that was his, for in his journal he commented, "No one who has not commanded an expedition of this kind, where everything ahead is dim, uncertain, and unknown, except the dangers, can imagine the anxiety with which I start upon this journey." He knew that he was responsible not only "for the lives of my men" but also for his own reputation and the "highest wrought expectations of my friends, and the still more highly wrought expectations of envious enemies. . . ."

Beale rejoined the caravan at the pueblo of Zuñi on August 29, and with these Indians he traded for corn to feed his horses and mules. It was packed on the camels, about 700 pounds each. Across the Little Colorado they went, moving west to camp on September 5 near the present Holbrook, Arizona, beside an ancient Indian pueblo. In the high desert country there, it was cold at night, but the camels moved steadily along. Beale's admiration for these animals had attained almost a lyrical quality as he wrote in his journal:

> The camels are so quiet and give so little trouble, that sometimes we forget they are with us. Certainly there never was anything so patient and enduring and so little troublesome as this noble animal. They pack their heavy load of corn, of which they never taste a grain; put up with any food offered them without complaint, and are always up with the wagons, and, withal, so perfectly docile and

A general view of Fort Defiance, New Mexico, as seen by Edward F. Beale. *Courtesy U. S. Signal Corps, National Archives.*

quiet that they are the admiration of the whole camp. . . . At this time there is not a man in camp who is not delighted with them.

Actually this expedition was not breaking new ground or moving into unknown country, for they had with them the map made by Lieutenant Amiel Weeks Whipple, who in 1853 had surveyed a railroad route along the 35th parallel. Yet in mid-September Beale's guide became confused and led the party into a dead-end canyon where there was neither water nor grass. Beale was livid, saying of the guide, "I ought to have killed him there, but I did not." Beale suddenly realized he was at a place thirty-two miles from water and "in a country entirely unknown." He sent two men east on camels to hunt water, while he led a party mounted on horses to the west. When he finally returned to camp, it was to learn that the men on camels had found the Little Colorado River some sixteen to twenty miles away, but in extremely rough country. By this time the animals had been without water for thirty-six hours and were frantic. Beale noted that a group of horses and mules had congregated around "a small barrel of water and trying to drink from the bung hole, . . . seemingly frantic with distress and eagerness to get at it." However, the "camels appeared to view this proceeding with great contempt, and kept quietly browsing on the grass and bushes." Even Stacey was moved to commend the camels, although only slightly; he noted that they had little to drink for many hours, saying, "It is a remarkable thing how they stood it so well as they did, traveling under a hot sun all day and packing . . . [several] hundred pounds apiece."

By this time young Stacey and the others in the expedition thought of themselves as real Westerners—and perhaps were growing a bit careless, or so Beale thought on September 26. Returning quietly to the camp beside King's Creek that evening about 10:00 p.m., he found a campfire burning but no one apparently on guard. "I determined to frighten them," he wrote, "so drawing my revolver, and giving two or three Indian yells, I fired

"Watering the animals upon finding a stream," a painting by Narjot. *Courtesy U. S. Signal Corps, National Archives.*

it off." His horse did not understand the joke, however, and taking the bit between its teeth the animal wheeled and ran for several miles. Finally it stumbled and "with a tremendous crash that made me see stars, we came down together." Fortunately for Beale, the animal's feet were entangled in the bridle and did not dash off. Beale was so stunned that he "remained bruised on the ground until nearly morning." Finally recovering somewhat, he rode slowly back to camp only to discover a further humiliation. When he had ridden into the camp the previous night, the campfire he had seen burning with no guards around it was at a camp already abandoned. Beale declared this event most "mortifying."

In the real camp, Beale's "joke" brought confusion and a near stampede of the horses and mules. However, the camels stayed quiet, exhibiting one more point in their favor—they were almost impossible to stampede. Beale appreciated this, noting in his journal,

> My admiration for the camels increases daily with my experience of them. The harder the test they are put to the more fully they seem to justify all that can be said of them. They pack water for others four days under a hot sun and never get a drop; they pack heavy burdens of corn and oats for months and never get a grain; and on bitter greasewood and other worthless shrubs not only subsist but keep fat; withal, they are so perfectly docile and so admirably contented with whatever fate befalls them. No one could do justice to their merits or value in expeditions of this kind, and I look forward to the day when every mail route across the continent will be conducted and worked altogether with this economical and noble brute.

Westward they continued, meeting some Indians along the way, but peacefully. In some places during their descent down the mountains toward the Colorado River they found it necessary to unhitch their mules and guide their wagons on steep passes by rope. Then on October 17, just as they arrived at their designation, Mojave Indians swarmed into the camp. "They are a fine-looking, comfortable, fat and merry set," Beale wrote of them. Soon the Americans were surrounded, and attempts at conversation were made. Some of the Mojaves apparently had met other

Americans, for one of them saluted Beale with what he had learned, "God damn my soul eyes. How de do! How de do." The following day these Indians returned to trade melons, corn, and beans for wornout shirts, handkerchiefs, and almost any item in the camp. However, it was not the Indians who fared worst in this trade, for Beale commented, "They are shrewder at a bargain, though, than our men, whose keen appetites [for fresh food] cannot bear the delay necessary to a successful trade." He and his men found watermelons, cantaloupes, and pumpkins, for which they traded a real treat after months of beans, salt pork, and other such delights.

Crossing the Colorado River proved difficult, but less than Beale had anticipated. He had been told that camels could not swim, and he thought this was confirmed when the first camel led to the river's edge refused to take to the water. He then ordered the largest, finest camel brought forward, whereupon it plunged in and easily swam "across the rapidly flowing river." He then had the camels lined up and tied "one to the saddle of another, and without the slightest difficulty, in a short time swam them all to the opposite side in gangs, five in a gang." To Beale's delight they not only swam with ease, "but with apparently more strength than horses or mules." All landed safely on the west bank.[10] Not so with the horses and mules. Two horses and ten mules drowned in the attempt, but these were not wasted; Stacey noted tersely, "Indians ate the drowned ones."

Writing to the secretary of war on October 18, Beale wrote his report on the experiment—and was as lavish in his praise to Floyd as he had been in his journal. He summarized his own feelings when he noted that at the start of the expedition his men had not been favorable toward the camel, but by the end of the trek "there is not one of them who would not prefer the most indifferent of our camels to four of our best mules." The expedition of more than 100 animals, twelve wagons, and forty-four men had succeeded in surveying a wagon road from Fort Defiance to the Colorado River across the 35th parallel.[11]

There on the Colorado River (fifteen miles north of the present Needles, California), Beale had to decide his destination from that point. At first he thought of sending Stacey and three companions down the Colorado to Fort Yuma to assess the navigability of the river, but changed his mind. Instead he chose to follow his orders, which stated that "in the event of a want of provisions, to proceed to Fort Tejon and procure them there." Happily for Beale, Fort Tejon was very near Tejon Ranch, a property he had acquired while Indian superintendent for California. The rest of that trek was not recorded either in Stacey's journal or in Beale's official report. Rather Beale noted that he followed "the United States surveyor's trail from the river to Los Angeles."

Actually he separated his party, taking two camels to Los Angeles and sending the rest, along with his wagons and other animals, directly to Fort Tejon. With Hi-Jolly and a party of eight others, Beale mounted Seid, Hi-Jolly rode another camel named Tuili, and the rest were on horseback. Following the stagecoach road, they came through Cajon Pass to San Bernardino, arriving at Los Angeles on November 9, 1857, causing great excitement in the little village. Horses reared and dashed about, throwing Mexican horsemen to the delight of everyone. Two days later the party set out for Fort Tejon.

Fort Tejon had been created three years previously to protect the Indians at the San Sebastian Reservation from intruding whites. Opened on June 24, 1854, it housed a company of infantry and another of dragoons, but no permanent quarters were built; rather the men were housed in tents. Beale, reporting to the post now and then from his ranch at El Tejon, chose to keep the camels away from the post. They were sent into the nearby Sierra Nevadas where snow was on the ground to test the effect of cold weather on them. They suffered not at all from it, seeming, in fact, to enjoy it. And when a wagon loaded with supplies for Fort Tejon became stuck in the snow and ice, camels were sent to the rescue; where six mules had been unable to move, the dromedaries had no difficulty.

On January 6, 1858, Beale took fourteen camels and twenty men to test in winter the road he had just surveyed, proceeding first to Los Angeles. There a reporter for the *San Francisco Evening*

Bulletin recorded his impressions, which were published on January 25:

> Gen. Beale and about fourteen camels stalked into town last Friday week and gave our streets quite an Oriental aspect. It looked oddly enough to see, outside of a menagerie, a herd of huge ungainly awkward but docile animals move about in our midst with people riding them like horses. . . . These camels under charge of General Beale are all grown and serviceable and most of them are well broken to the saddle and are very gentle. . . . These animals are admirably adapted to travel across our continent and their introduction was a brilliant idea the result of which is beginning most happily. . . . Their drivers say they will get fat where a jackass would starve to death.

Apparently Beale crossed the Mojave Desert without incident, for he gave the trip only half a sentence in his journal. However, at the Colorado River occurred a bizarre accidental meeting to which he devoted more space. "Here, in a wild, almost unknown country, inhabited only by savages, the great river of the west, hitherto declared unnavigable, had, for the first time borne upon its bosom that emblem of civilization, a steamer," he wrote. There on the banks of the Colorado on January 23, 1858, Beale met Captain George Alonso Johnson, who had steamed upriver in the *General Jessup.*

Johnson had pioneered steam service on the Colorado, founding his own firm in 1853 to operate between Fort Yuma and the Gulf of California. With the onset of the so-called Mormon War in 1857, agents of the federal government approached Johnson about attempting to open navigation much farther up the river in order to supply troops being sent west to Utah. Johnson replied that he wanted $3500 a month to charter his boat. The War Department considered this amount excessive and proceeded to spend $75,000 to build its own boat, the *Explorer,* in Philadelphia, knock it apart, and send it around the Horn to the Gulf of California for reassembly. Johnson, meanwhile, had determined to be first up the Colorado, and with no subsidy he steamed upriver—where he encountered Beale and the camels.[12]

No photograph of the *General Jessup* is known; however, the *Cocopah*, a similar vessel, shows that steamers on the Colorado River of the West were not floating pleasure palaces. *From the Arizona Historical Society.*

A few minutes after Beale arrived at the Colorado, the steamer pulled up to the bank, took them and their baggage aboard, and ferried them across the river. Beale admitted that the entire scene was strange: the camels standing on the bank, hundreds of Indians milling about, dragoons in uniform mixed with them, and a steamboat slowly revolving its sternwheel. He understood that this event meant great changes for the area, especially for the Mojave Indians: ". . . Alas! for the poor Indians living on its banks. . . . The steam whistle of the 'General Jessup' sounded the death knell of the river race."

At this point the camels were returned to Fort Tejon, Beale continuing eastward after swimming his mules across the river. Already he noted that the road he had surveyed the previous autumn was in use by Indians. By February 19, after fighting snowstorms and cold weather, the party was at Inscription Rock (El Moro) near the Zuñi villages of western New Mexico. Finally they arrived at the point where the survey had begun seven months before, and Beale was moved to write with pride—and some egotism—of what he had accomplished:

> A year in the wilderness ended! During this time I have conducted my party from the Gulf of Mexico to the shores of the Pacific Ocean, and back again to the eastern terminus of the road, through a country for a great part entirely unknown, and inhabited by hostile Indians, without the loss of a man. I have tested the value of the camels, marked a new road to the Pacific, and travelled 4,000 miles without an accident.

From this point Beale proceeded to Washington, arriving there in April of 1858 to make his report to Secretary of War Floyd.[13] When this report got to the hands of Quartermaster General Thomas S. Jesup, he was sufficiently thoughtful to forward a copy to Major Henry C. Wayne, who at that time was attached to the Office of Army Clothing and Equipage in Philadelphia. Wayne was delighted to note Beale's success, replying to Jesup, "It is gratifying to know that our experiment is sustained by actual use and practical demonstration, and that what we told the people through the press and through Congress, of the capabilities of the Camel and of its adaptation to our country, should be realized as truth." [14]

While these experiments had been transpiring in California, Captain Innis N. Palmer had been trying to secure funds with which to pay the expenses of the camels yet under his care at Camp Verde. As usual, his superiors in the Army were moving very slowly. On July 31, 1857, he wrote that he had requested such funds be authorized on the previous May 20 and again on July 6. The result, he wrote, was that he was "every day placed in a most disagreeable situation." Some of those who had been employed to erect the buildings at Camp Verde had tried to sell their claims against the government for whatever they could get, and Palmer had been so embarrassed that he had advanced $1100 out of his own pocket to settle these "just debts." Making matters worse was the severe drought in Texas that year, in consequence of which little work was to be had by laborers. Suffering even more were the "Turks and Greeks" imported to work with the camels; these men, Palmer wrote, had "become nearly naked."

Despite his troubles, however, Palmer had become interested in the camels in his care. "I have done everything I could in assisting to develop a grand experiment," he wrote. "My time and attention have been cheerfully given to the subject without hope of reward in any way. . . ." Inasmuch as Beale had taken the twenty-five choice camels, he was left with forty-six other animals—and no funds. He still had one man working as interpreter and overseer, along with five drovers. Because the drovers had not been paid for several months, they had refused to work any longer, whereupon Palmer had threatened to "flog the whole party"; this "brought to terms" the drovers, but did not end the basic problem of paying them.[15]

Assuming command of the Department of Texas that summer of 1857 was Brevet Major General David E. Twiggs, a crusty veteran of the War of 1812 who saw little reason to innovate. Born in Georgia in 1790, he had been appointed a captain of infantry on March 12, 1812. After that war ended, he remained in the Army, rising steadily and attaining the rank of brigadier general on June 30, 1846. Shortly afterward he was breveted a major general for his brave conduct at the Battle of Monterrey, even receiving, by resolution of Congress, a presentation sword for "his gallantry and good conduct in storming Monterrey." [16]

At his headquarters in San Antonio, Twiggs was astonished to

General David E. Twiggs. *Courtesy U. S. Signal Corps* (*Brady Collection*), *National Archives*.

find that within his department was a detachment of camels, and he demanded additional information from the local quartermaster. Major D. H. Vinton, who held that office, immediately wrote Lieutenant W. P. Chambliss, quartermaster at Camp Verde, for "information respecting the camels at Camp Verde." Chambliss responded on September 10, stating that the number of camels there, both young and old, was thirty-four old and twelve young. These dromedaries occasionally had been used for trips to San Antonio to fetch forage. Still employed with the project at that time were "one Camel Master at forty-five Dollars per month and four drivers at twenty dollars per month each."

General Twiggs wrote an extremely abrupt endorsement on this as he forwarded it to the Assistant Adjutant General of the Army: "I have seen but little of these camels, but, from what I have seen, I would much prefer mules for packing." [17]

Three months later, in January 1858, the crusty old general was even more adamant in a letter to Quartermaster General Jesup. Concerning the camels, he wrote, "They are not under my control and Major Vinton says they are not in his; he has only to pay the money on requisition of Captain Palmer. As these animals render no service in this Department, I trust their expense will not be included in that of this Department." He concluded, his pen dripping irony, "According to some accounts of the road makers, which I have seen in the newspapers, they never eat nor drink; if such is the fact, they had all better be sent on the roads, as at Camp Verde, the Quarter-Master informs me, the full forage ration of grain is issued to them." [18]

No one seemed to know what to do with the animals, not Twiggs, not Jesup—certainly not Captain Palmer at Camp Verde. Yet on him fell the responsibility for caring for them and for paying the drovers imported to care for them. And the herd was presenting a new problem. In October, while Twiggs was writing a recommendation to rid himself of the camels, Palmer was addressing himself to Quartermaster General Jesup to say that the camels were well and healthy, that the young camels were growing rapidly, and that soon it would be necessary to build an addition to the stables at Camp Verde because the young dromedaries were requiring as much room as the older ones. [19]

The Becharieh dromedary as drawn by Gwinn Harris Heap.

Palmer's trial finally ended on May 3, 1858, when he received orders to move with his regiment to Fort Leavenworth, Kansas. Immediately he sent a telegram to Secretary of War Floyd asking instructions: "What can I do with them?" he asked plaintively; "The commanding officer of the Department of Texas can give me no information." [20] This telegram evidently produced results, for on June 26 Major D. H. Vinton, quartermaster at San Antonio, wrote Quartermaster General Jesup that he was in receipt of orders commending the camels to his "especial care and supervision" as of June 1. Vinton's duties prevented his visiting Camp Verde until late in the month, after which he reported he had no fault to find, only a recommendation to place the animals under the care of a civilian who would receive a salary of $100 per month. [21] Apparently this recommendation produced an unfavorable response, for on July 8 Vinton wrote General Jesup that Lieutenant William M. Graham, assistant quartermaster at Camp Verde, had been assigned responsibility for the camels. [22]

At Camp Verde the camels little cared who was in charge so long as they were fed regularly. One animal died in June, but four more were born. Vinton noted wryly that the climate and pasturage at Camp Verde seemed particularly favorable for the propagation of the camel species. At this point General Jesup, by letter on July 21, suggested that Captain Palmer might be returned to Texas to take charge of the animals. Vinton responded that General Twiggs had "cogent reasons" and "*positive* objections" to the return of Palmer; apparently Palmer somehow had angered Twiggs. While these officers fussed politely behind high-flown salutations and closed with "Your Obedient Servant," Lieutenant Graham kept the camels at Camp Verde fed—and watched them increase in numbers.

By the spring of 1858 no one in the Army seemed to know what to do with the dromedaries that had been imported. Almost fifty of the animals were at Camp Verde, while another twenty-five were at Fort Tejon, California, yet permanent assignment of the beasts had been made. Everyone who had used them in the field had been unstinting in his praise of what the camel could accomplish, but the central question remained: what was to be the future of the animal in America? The soldiers and civilians most closely associated with the dromedaries had viewed them as admirable bearers of freight and of dispatches. But in Washington, D.C., where policy was set, the secretary of war saw them as useful for military purposes.

John B. Floyd, in his first annual message as secretary of war, commented that he had sent Edward Fitzgerald Beale to survey a wagon road. "From the recent reports received from Mr Beale," he wrote, "it would appear that the camels are likely to answer fully the high expectations entertained of them *for military purposes* [italics added] by the honorable Secretary who introduced them into the country [Jefferson Davis]." [23]

A year later, in his second report—made after Beale had completed his work—Secretary of War Floyd was even more enthusiastic: "The entire adaptation of camels *to military operations* [italics added] upon the plains may now be taken as demonstrated, whilst their great usefulness and superiority in many particulars is equally certain." He thought the dromedary would enable soldiers to move rapidly in pursuit of roving bands of Indians and thereby catch and punish the marauders. Eventually, he thought, the superiority of the camel over the horse would convince the Indians that they could never escape by flight and therefore would cease their raiding. Thus he recommended that Congress, as a measure of "wise economy," should authorize the purchase of 1000 camels. He concluded by transmitting with his report a treatise on the camel written by Hekekyan Bey of Cairo, Egypt. This study, essentially about military uses of the camel, was printed in both the House and Senate versions of his report. [24]

If high officials in the War Department seemingly were uncertain about what to do with the camels, many civilians were not. During these years the secretary of war was bombarded with letters from various individuals, each in some way hoping to profit from the camel experiment. For example, Richard Meade of Texas applied in May of 1858 to be placed in charge of the camel depot at Camp Verde; unselfishly he wrote "to offer myself as a candidate" for this job. [25]

However, most civilians wished to supply camels to the Army

should additional animals be imported. Among the most persistent of these was William L. Cazneau, also of Texas. Writing on August 29, 1857, he first declared his interest in the "rapid development of our South Western steppes as well as to the increased efficiency of the United States transportation service"; apparently this was a reference to the quartermaster function. He and other interested parties in New York City, he said, were "disposed to make arrangements for the extensive and systematic importation of the hardy North African camel." What he and the "interested parties" wished was that the government would show "some evidence of good will" for this enterprise—which meant buying "one or two hundred animals" from them. Again on January 19, 1858, he wrote, this time from Washington, to say that the government had never tested the camel in the Southwest "fully and fairly." He proposed, therefore, to supply the Army with "any required number, from one hundred, onward" at a price of $300 per head.

Still not receiving the order he wanted, Cazneau wrote again on January 27, this time trying to bring political pressure to bear. He asserted that the Texas congressional delegation "will assure you of the interest and satisfaction that State will feel at the full introduction of the camel in the South West." With this solicitation he included a copy of a letter he recently had received from Jefferson Davis, the ex-secretary of war, but this was little more than an extension of best wishes for Cazneau to succeed in establishing "a park for these animals in Texas." Cazneau continued his own letter by stating that he was willing to enter into a contract with the War Department to import dromedaries "subject to the contingency of Congress ratifying the contract, or making an appropriation for their purchase." His price still was $300 per head.[26]

G. B. Lamar of Savannah, Georgia, likewise wanted to contract with the War Department to furnish camels. "I am desirous to contract to furnish . . . Camels imported from Africa," he wrote on January 26, 1858. He said he had a ship ready to sail under command of his thirty-year-old son, who personally would select the camels to be imported. And on February 8, 1858, E. R.

Ware of New York City wrote to say that he was engaged in trade with Africa and that he was prepared to import camels for the War Department "from the Morocco Coast." His price was $400 apiece.[27]

Strangest of all these letters, however, was one from "James J. Fisher & Sons" of Baltimore. Fisher wrote that he daily was expecting at New York a shipment "from Guayaquil, via Panama" of approximately 100 llamas and alpacas; these he hoped to sell in the United States "as well because of the value of their wool, as from their usefulness as beasts for carrying burdens in mountainous districts impracticable to other animals." In addition, the llama and alpaca, he asserted, were noted for their ability to withstand fatigue "under an economical allowance of food and water." Inasmuch as the War Department was testing camels, he thought officers there might also be interested in purchasing some of the new animals for tests.[28]

Simultaneously there were a few requests coming to the War Department from Army officers in the West who wanted to use the camels already imported for experiments of a purely military nature. One such individual was Captain Richard S. Ewell. He originally had been ordered to southern Arizona late in 1856, there to command the troops at Fort Buchanan, a post located near Tucson in the heart of the desert country. While in Santa Fe, Ewell on October 12, 1857, wrote an official request for camels to be sent to his post, which he considered "a point well adapted to their use." He noted, doubtless tongue-in-cheek, that the climate of the Gadsden Purchase area was "mild and equable," and that the roads generally were "dry and level—the face of the country being mountain ranges divided by dry plains." He stated that while on campaigns in the past his soldiers had been forced to leave the roads to pursue Indians over mountains and across deserts, and that on such marches the horses and mules had suffered severely from want of water. His desire was to experiment in the vicinity of Fort Buchanan both with "express" and "burden" camels. However, if only one or two dromedaries could be sent him, he definitely preferred the express camel

A typical Army pack train, this one in Arizona, which Henry C. Wayne and other enthusiasts hoped the camel would replace. *From the Arizona Historical Society.*

"as most likely to be of important service." In short, Ewell wanted to mount his men on camels to ride in pursuit of raiding Indians.

Such a test as Ewell proposed would have afforded the War Department an excellent opportunity to test the camel "for military purposes," as Congress had phrased the purpose of the experiment. And Ewell was an ideal candidate for the experiment, for he was an excellent officer. The Quartermaster officer who endorsed this request at Santa Fe stated that he knew of no one "who will take more interest in the subject and who will exercise better judgement in the management of the camels than Capt. Ewell." [29]

This request received as little consideration as had those from private citizens wanting to import dromedaries for the War Department—leading to the conclusion that Secretary of War Floyd was not entirely certain in his own mind what the future of the Camel Corps was to be.

6
CAMELS IN CALIFORNIA AND TEXAS

Secretary of War John B. Floyd had little time to reflect on the proper use for the camels that had been imported, for by 1858 officials in Washington were almost totally consumed with more momentous affairs. Kansas had been much in the news since 1854 as Jayhawkers and Bushwhackers sniped at the other from ambush and "Bleeding Kansas" became synonymous with the hatreds of abolitionists and pro-slavery people. In 1857 the Supreme Court had reached its famed Dred Scott decision which, in effect, meant that slavery was legal everywhere in the country. This wave of tension was not lessened by the debates between Abraham Lincoln and Stephen A. Douglas in 1858. In this era when hatreds inflamed reason and men of passion held the national spotlight, determining a philosophy for the Camel Corps had a low priority.

Therefore the herds at Camp Verde, Texas, and Fort Tejon, California, were assigned no major duties. Despite the continuing complaints of General Davis Twiggs, commanding the Department of Texas, the camels at Camp Verde occasionally came to San Antonio for a load of supplies, and funds had to be sent every month to pay the drovers associated with the project. In California they were sent now and then to Los Angeles for provisions; for example, the *Los Angeles Star* reported on July 21, 1858, "The camels, eight in number, came into town from Fort Tejon, after provisions for that camp. The largest ones pack a ton and can travel sixteen miles an hour." The public belief about dromedaries was so exaggerated that apparently no one wrote the *Star* to complain about this overstatement of the speed and carrying capacity of the animal.

Beale, meanwhile, was approached in Washington about accepting yet another road-making assignment, this time from Fort Smith, Arkansas, westward to connect with the one made on his previous trek. Once at Fort Smith, Beale hired Jesse Chisholm, a part-Cherokee later to be known for the cattle trail he helped popularize, and Black Beaver, a Delaware, as guides. From Fort Smith the party made its way west along the Canadian River, eventually reaching the Rio Grande; later Beale estimated that a railroad could be built along his route for $21,391,100 (later the Rock Island would put tracks along this route from Little Rock, Arkansas, to Tucumcari, New Mexico). In January, Beale conducted an "official visit to Santa Fé, and a social one to my old and esteemed friend Kit Carson." Surveying in New Mexico filled February, then Beale began trekking westward once more to complete his task of connecting with the road previously surveyed.

Inasmuch as he could carry with him only enough supplies to reach the Colorado River, he sent one of his men, F. C. Kerlin, to California by way of El Paso to ask that provisions be brought to the Colorado to be waiting for him there, along with an escort of soldiers. Troops were desirable because immigrants using the wagon road across the 35th parallel had been attacked the previous August. The Army in California found that no troops could be at the Colorado when Beale arrived, but S. A. Bishop, who was using the camels for contract hauling for the Army in California, gathered forty frontiersmen, loaded supplies on camels, and hurried to the aid of Beale and his party.

At the Colorado, Bishop was confronted "by a thousand warriors flushed with their success over the emigrants, and rendered confident by their skirmish with the troops." Yet the forty frontiersmen with Bishop fought so ferociously that the Indians soon fled the field of battle, whereupon the party from California crossed the Colorado and boldly and defiantly occupied the natives' village. Bishop then divided his men sending twenty back to Los Angeles, leaving six at the Indian village, and, with the other fourteen mounted on camels, riding east to meet Beale. Two days later the fourteen were attacked by 200 "choice warriors, anxious to wipe out the disgrace of their late defeat." Again Bishop was victorious, after which he was joined by two mail riders who had been trying fruitlessly for nearly a year to cross the region.

The two parties met at Leroux Springs (near the present Flagstaff, Arizona). As Bishop's group rode in, Beale from a distance recognized Seid, the great white dromedary he had ridden previously, and mounted on another camel was Hadji Ali (Hi Jolly), who had remained with the animals at Fort Tejon. The eastbound mail was given to the postal employee riding with Beale, and he returned to New Mexico, while the westbound mail was transferred to camelback and went on to California by that method. Beale proudly wrote, "Thus the first mail of the 35th parallel was brought on my camels both ways. . . ." The next day after this meeting, April 20, Beale noted in his report, "Our camels with their solemn faces make our camp look like old times again."

Continuing to the Colorado River, the expedition found the Mojave Indians hostile—and learned that a detachment of soldiers, who had reached the area, had appropriated the supplies brought from California. Leaving their men there, Beale and Bishop with three camels left for Fort Tejon on May 4 for additional provisions. He returned on June 26, crossed the Colorado, and began a return trip to Albuquerque with his men, improving the wagon road as he went. From New Mexico, Beale returned to Washington to make his report, and then went to Chester, Pennsylvania, to rest. He had completed his thirteenth crossing of the plains—but he had not ended his connection with the camels.[1]

Commanding the Department of California at this time was

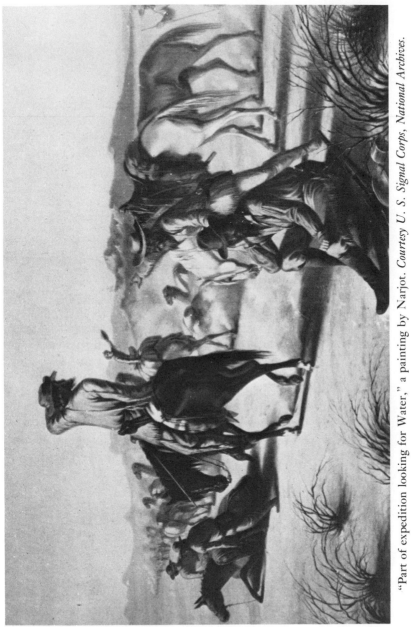

"Part of expedition looking for Water," a painting by Narjot. *Courtesy U. S. Signal Corps, National Archives.*

Brevet Brigadier General Newman S. Clarke. From San Francisco on February 4, 1859, he had written to Quartermaster General Thomas S. Jesup to say that he had been informed of camels in Southern California; he wanted these animals assigned to him for use, "in solving the difficult problem of supporting a post on the Upper Colorado," for such supplies would have to be carried across the desert. General Jesup accordingly referred the request to Secretary of War Floyd, stating that the animals currently were "supported by the Quartermaster Department and are a dead weight upon the Department." Therefore he wanted them transferred to General Clarke, "who will be able to test their efficiency for the military service in the desert portion of our territory." [2]

The wheels of the bureaucracy turned slowly, however, and the camels continued that summer of 1859 and into the fall to be under the direction of S. A. Bishop, a civilian partner of Edward Fitzgerald Beale. Not until November 19 were the animals formally turned over to the Army; on that date Lieutenant H. R. Davidson, a quartermaster assigned to the 1st Dragoons, took charge of them. By this time the animals numbered twenty-eight. Davidson complained that they were "in a very poor condition, many of their backs being very sore." Apparently one camel was missing, for Davidson, in his report, noted "There is one deficiency, and can no where be found." Davidson reported that he had hired two men to care for the animals, "a Turk and a Greek"; these two men were Hadji Ali and Georgis Caralambo, better known as Hi Jolly and Greek George. Both of them had gone west with Beale on the original survey.

Employing these camels did prove expensive. Lieutenant Davidson sent, with his letter, an estimate of the funds required to maintain these animals for November and December, 1859, and January and February 1860. A herder would get thirty dollars per month, while barley and hay would total $1583.88. Brevet Major J. H. Carleton, commander of Fort Tejon, was happy, however, writing in his endorsement,

> I am very glad the Service has at length secured these camels. The experiment of rearing, subsisting, and employing them, whether

with profit or otherwise, can doubtless be more thoroughly and fairly tested in this Military Department than in any other in this country. In moving with a small force over our deserts, or for explorations of new routes, &c., where there are doubts about finding water from day to day, they will be invaluable.[3]

The experiment at Fort Tejon never proved as valuable as Major Carleton hoped. Not long after the animals came under Lieutenant Davidson's care, fifteen of them escaped during a rainstorm. Searchers found nine of them near San Bernardino, and the other six were recovered near Lake Elizabeth. Then in 1860 Captain W. S. Hancock was given permission to establish a "camel express" between Los Angeles and Fort Mohave, a distance of approximately 300 miles. Wagons pulled by mules previously had made this trip in sixteen to eighteen days, or else goods were sent by ship from Los Angeles around Baja California to the mouth of the Colorado; there they were transferred to river steamboat and went up to Fort Yuma, after which they moved by wagon to posts in northern Arizona and inland California. Hancock argued that he could deliver these goods to Fort Mohave cheaper and quicker by camelback.

Greek George set out on September 21, 1860, for the inauguration of what the newspapers hailed as the "Dromedary Line." Yet that first trip proved a failure when the camel died "of exhaustion." Naturally the unknown journalist writing the story could not resist using nautical terms to speak of the incident: "This 'ship of the desert' foundered 'at sea' last week, going down with all hands." He concluded that "the old mules still keep in favor." [4] The Dromedary Line itself died after a few more trips.[5]

The camels were used more successfully—but by civilians—on the survey of the California boundary north from Mexico to Lake Tahoe. On August 17, 1860, Sylvester Mowry, wrote Secretary of War Floyd asking that he be authorized to "use the camels in such numbers of them as may be of service" to him. He noted that the country through which the survey would be passing was of such a nature as to make their employment "of great service" and would demonstrate again "the successful experiment initiated by the War Department." This former Army lieutenant had served at Fort Yuma in 1856 before resigning, and previous to that had been in Utah; therefore he was familiar with the desert country—both of which inclined Floyd to agree with the request. Replying on September 4, the secretary of war instructed the Quartermaster Office in California to make available "camels, not to exceed ten, as the commissioner, Mr. Sylvester Mowry, may require." [6]

By the time Mowry arrived in California, he found that the camels had been moved from Fort Tejon, which was to be closed, to Camp Fitzgerald in Los Angeles. At first the animals were housed in a stable attached to the quartermaster's office on Main Street, but later they were moved to another stable on Second Street. Hi Jolly and Greek George, their keepers, could be seen almost every day giving rides to the more daring school children while their fearful companions looked on through the fence.

After Mowry's arrival and before he could leave, two of the camels, Seid and Tuili, began fighting. Naturally this occurred during the rutting season, and the two males fought so furiously that no one dared try to separate them. Seid was pushed to the ground, as was normal for the loser in such fights, but Tuili then stepped on his head and crushed it. Mowry secured the bones of this large animal and forwarded them to the Smithsonian Institution.

On January 13, 1861, while this boundary commission was yet in Los Angeles, it was encamped beside a river. Suddenly the river flooded and swept away "their tents, saddles, equipage, all—one camel killed." [7] In February, Mowry sent three camels to Dr. J. R. N. Owen at Fort Mohave; Owen's task was to take fourteen men and establish a number of depots in which supplies were to be stored for Mowry's surveying party. These depots were to be in "the terrific desert country between the 35th and the 37th parallels" between Fort Mohave and Lake Tahoe. Hi Jolly came out with the camels, which, when they departed from Fort Mohave, were loaded with 1400 pounds of supplies. [8]

Later that same year, between October and December, Hi Jolly rode camels to carry dispatches between Los Angeles and Fort Yuma. In order to keep this express moving regularly, some of the camels were transferred to Fort Yuma. Other of the ani-

American soldier in California attempting to ride a camel while Hi Jolly watches. *Courtesy California Section, California State Library.*

mals were sent to San Pedro, then the principal seaport for Los Angeles, and were used to transport freight between the two towns. Yet, in truth, most of the government's camels in California were underemployed, a fact all too apparent to Edward Fitzgerald Beale, who returned to the state in 1861 as United States Surveyor-General for California and Nevada. He wrote the new secretary of war, Edwin M. Stanton, asking that the entire camel herd in California be turned over to him; he promised to give the animals proper care at his El Tejon ranch and to employ them in his survey work. Stanton then was too involved in the Civil War to worry about approximately thirty camels in California and ignored the request. Thus in 1861, as the great war began, the Army's camels in California were scattered at several posts where few officers or men appreciated them.

The arrival of the camels in California with Edward Fitzgerald

Beale after his survey of a wagon road in 1857 caused some civilians to conclude that the dromedary might solve many problems of transportation in that state. In fact, the year before the editor of the Stockton *Argus* had printed a long editorial in which he extolled the virtues of the animals; the editorial, reprinted in the San Francisco *Herald* on December 13, 1856, asserted, "The next move in our progress of improvement should be the introduction of camels in California. . . . It is capable of traveling over one hundred miles per day—is known to live to a green old age, as long as seventy or eighty years—to go without eating or drinking for four or five days—to be able to carry twice the load of our largest and most hardy mules."

On May 13, 1859, ten men in Downieville incorporated the California and Utah Camel Association. The charter stated that the Association was capitalized at $12,000 with 120 shares valued at $100 each, and that its purpose was "the introduction, and employment of the Camel on the Pacific Coast." Apparently nothing other than articles of incorporation came of this effort, although the charter was not forfeited until December 13, 1905; the state that year had passed a license tax of ten dollars on all corporations in the state, those not paying it to lose their license.[9]

Otto Esche, a merchant in San Francisco, was more ambitious. In 1860 he traveled to China to secure camels which he intended to use to transport supplies and ore in California's mining country. Because he thought camels from a colder climate would fare better in the mountains, he journeyed to the Amur country of Mongolia and there purchased thirty-two Bactrians. However, seventeen of the animals perished on the way to the nearest seaport; the other fifteen did complete the trip aboard the *Caroline E. Foote,* a cargo vessel, which docked at San Francisco on July 25, 1860. Esche sent another sixteen camels to San Francisco aboard the same ship, animals from Tartary, in 1861. And he purchased another forty-two camels in Siberia and shipped them aboard a German ship, the *Dollart;* however, the animals were so crowded on this vessel that twenty-four of them died at sea. Esche sued the captain of the *Dollart* and was awarded $260 for each of the dead animals. Thus of the ninety camels Esche had purchased and started toward the United States, forty-five died en route.

Those Bactrians that did arrive were in sad condition, their humps "shriveled down to mere skinny sacks, which hung in flabby ugliness over their sides." Esche first rested and fed the animals until they presented a better appearance, after which they were placed on exhibit; advertisements stated that a native drover from the Gobi Desert would display their many talents and abilities—admission adults fifty cents, children twenty-five cents. After almost two weeks in a tent on Bush Street, the exhibition was moved to the Agricultural Fair, after which they were put up for auction, Esche hoping to recover $1200 per camel. Unfortunately for him the highest bid received was $475 for one animal, whereupon he announced that he would sell them separately.

Ten Bactrians subsequently were purchased by Julius Bandman, who kept them in a pasture on Pacific Street. Occasionally he drove the animals to the Presidio to allow them to graze on thistles, which they seemed to like and which grew there in quantity. After testing the animals to see what loads they could carry comfortably, Bandman sent nine of the animals overland to pack salt to the Washoe silver mills in Esmeralda County.

Esche sold another twenty-three of his camels to a mining company in British Columbia for $6000. Because the new owners feared for the animals' feet in the rugged mountains of Western Canada, they had the camels fitted with leather shoes, after which they sent them north to Douglas, British Columbia, to pack supplies into the Cariboo Mountains. This venture in 1862 did not prove profitable, and the disgusted Canadians turned the camels loose. Some of them reportedly made their way south into Idaho and eventually Nevada.[10]

While these events were transpiring in the Far West, civilians likewise were importing some animals into Texas—with even less success. Arriving at the port of Galveston on October 16, 1858, was the American ship *Thomas Watson*. The owner of the vessel, Mrs. M. J. Watson, declared to port authorities that she had aboard a cargo of eighty-nine camels valued at $9561 which she, a widow, wished to introduce into Texas; in the manner of Jefferson Davis, she was trying to pioneer a new form of transportation. Mrs. Watson next presented herself to the British consul at Galveston, Arthur T. Lynn, asking for clearance papers so she could take her vessel to Liverpool, England.

Lynn suspected that Mrs. Watson's true intentions were neither to import camels nor to go to Liverpool, however. The camels had been taken aboard the *Thomas Watson*, he thought, so that the strong smell of these animals would mask the odor typically associated with a vessel carrying slaves. He believed that Mrs. Watson actually intended to sail to Havana, Cuba, a notorious slave-trading port, and thus he declined to give the requested clean bill of health. His stated reason was the epidemic of yellow fever then ravaging Galveston, but in truth he had a strong moral aversion to slavery and wished to discourage this trade where possible.

Two months later Mrs. Watson was still in port, threatening to file protests with the American Department of State unless Lynn complied with her request, but always he found an excuse to refuse. Mrs. Watson thereupon hurried an urgent message to the person she called her "agent," but who actually was the owner of the *Thomas Watson*, to come at once from New York City where he resided.

Meanwhile the eighty-nine camels had been dumped ashore in Galveston to wander the streets. Young people in the town threw rocks at the animals, frightening them into rampages through the streets, whereupon the city fathers passed an ordinance declaring "That, from and after the passage of this ordinance, no person or person shall ride, drive, or introduce within the corporate limits of this city any camel or camels, except for the purpose of immediate shipment from the city." The penalty for breaking this new city law was a fine of not less than fifty dollars nor more than one hundred dollars "for each and every camel so ridden, driven, or introduced. . . ." [11]

Some of the stranded camels wandered outside the city limits to graze along the island itself. There some curious Galvestonians slaughtered a few of them out of a desire to try a "camel steak."

Other of the beasts died, doubtless from their long confinement aboard ship and the change in climate.[12] Mrs. Watson and her agent, J. A. Machado, apparently hoped to dispose of these animals by selling them to the government, a thought that left General David E. Twiggs, commanding the Department of Texas, aghast. To Quartermaster General Jesup he wrote most bluntly on December 22, 1858: "I see by the public prints some eighty camels have arrived at Galveston, and that they will be offered for sale to the United States as pack animals. I know but little about the fitness of camels for the Army, but those now at Verde do not transport their own forage. *I would not give one mule for five camels*—I do not object to the purchase of the camels, but I ask they may not be put in this Department for service." [13]

Into the situation in Galveston arrived Francis R. Lubbock, later to become a governor of Texas and owner of extensive land holdings outside Houston. Mrs. Watson by this time had managed to corral forty surviving camels and desperately was hunting for someone who would agree to care for the animals until they were "disposed of by sale or otherwise." Machado and Lubbock came to terms about what he would charge to pasture the animals and what his responsibilities were in caring for them. Machado then chartered a steamboat, the camels were taken aboard, and it steamed up Sims Bayou to deliver the herd at Lubbock's ranch. Once ashore the animals "showed their high spirits by jumping, rearing, and frisking about like sheep." Among the observers of this scene were Jules Baron, Lubbock's brother-in-law, and a Texan named Sam Allen. Baron commented that he thought no one could lasso a camel because of the animal's cavorting. Allen asserted the contrary, whereupon a ten-dollar bet was made between the two; the Texan thereupon mounted his horse, loosened his lasso, and on his first try roped a large camel and brought it crashing to the ground. Baron, only recently arrived from Louisiana, was astonished at such dexterity and paid the debt.

Machado left the camels, in Lubbock's words, in the care of "foreigners whom I will call 'Arabs.' " At Lubbock's ranch the animals were turned into a seventy-five-acre pasture bordered by a good fence, and there, in addition to the grass in the field, were given a good ration of cured hay. Every second or third day they were driven to a bayou to drink. Jules Victor Bouquet, who in 1857 had immigrated to Texas to settle at Indianola, later reminisced that he had observed the camels at Lubbock's ranch and remembered one getting bogged down in the bayou. He asked John Gonzales, one of the cowboys at the ranch, what was to be done. Gonzales replied that he would "pull out that camel." He managed to get his rope around the struggling animal, then tied it to another camel that had been saddled for the purpose. The trapped animal was pulled out and dragged across the mud to safe ground.[14] Lubbock commented about this difficulty with the camels that normally they were "drawn out of the bayou by a yoke of strong oxen; for after several ineffectual efforts to extricate themselves, and getting down deeper in the mire, they sank down quietly, with only a few mournful plaints of distress, apparently resigned to their fate." Only one animal died in the mud.

The animals had arrived during the winter, which was their rutting season, and thus the males were notoriously pugnacious. Nevertheless, people came from miles around to see the curious beasts, while one of the Arab drovers occasionally would ride a camel into Houston to fetch supplies; Lubbock noted of these trips into town that "their entry and exit would always create a sensation. One little girl in Houston at that time, Adele B. Looscan, recalled that she and a friend were given a ride when an animal came to town "equipped with the peculiar pack-saddle commonly used on these animals. . . . We rode about three-quarters of a mile, the camel being led by an Arab who trotted on ahead, continually encouraging the camel by ejaculations to which he seemed to respond." [15]

Late in March of 1859 Mrs. Watson and her agent, J. A. Machado, sailed away from Galveston. They never were able to secure a bill of health, nor were they able to sell the surviving camels to the government. Lubbock, when he stopped receiving funds from them for the care of the animals at his ranch, released the animals. Eventually most of them died of neglect or else were slaughtered by local citizens.[16] The reason why Texans hated these camels was because horses bolted in fright when they smelled a camel. John Rigsby of Beeville, Texas, recalled that when a boy, he and his father had been riding along the coast when their horses began snorting and prancing around. At first Rigsby's father thought a rattlesnake was in the vicinity, but on searching the area they found fresh camel prints in the sand. Apparently, however, some of the camels managed to exist for several years, for after the Civil War cowboys in the coastal region often chased a stray camel, trying to kill any they found.[17]

Either some of the camels turned loose by Lubbock wandered into the vicinity of Port Lavaca, Texas, or else a second shipment of the animals was brought in by some civilians. Mrs. L. E. Ward late in life recalled seeing a herd of "ten or twelve camels" at that city when they arrived there in 1859: "I was returning from school, my father having come after me, and he took me to a livery stable where two men were in charge of ten or twelve camels. Of course I was interested in them! Father asked me if I wanted to ride one. I did. He put me on a camel, and I rode it around the pen at the stable." [18]

While the civilians of Texas thus were having some pleasure, a little sport, and many vexations with the camels privately imported, Major General David E. Twiggs was still trying to divest his command of the animals at Camp Verde. His attitude toward the animals seemed to move from dislike to active hatred, for, when Mrs. Watson had tried to sell her animals to the government of the United States, he wrote Quartermaster General Jesup, *"I would not give one mule for five camels."* That letter of December 22, 1858, was followed slightly more than a month later by yet another in the same vein. To Jesup he complained that dromedaries would not "suit our soldiers.—they all understand mules." Moreover, he thought his command "too small" to conduct experiments. And he was skeptical about the claims he had read about the capabilities of the camel: *"I know* that no living animal can bear the pressure of six hundred pounds and go through a campaign in our country. Nineteen-twentieths of our mules, with the ordinary pack of one hundred and fifty or two hundred pounds, come out of a campaign with lacerated backs, and it takes months to cure them." His conclusion was equally blunt: "I do not want the camels in my command." [19]

On March 29 Twiggs tried another tactic to rid himself of the animals at Camp Verde—economy. "In these times of necessary economy," he wrote, "it becomes the duty of every officer having a command to see that the affairs of his command are managed with a view to the expenditure of public money." A place to cut in Texas, he thought, would be the dromedaries; "We have in this Department some forty or fifty camels; they are foraged and attended to at an expense of three hundred and ninety-five dollars a month. *Those animals render no service to the public,* nor are they likely to do so. . . ." For this reason he urged that they be transferred somewhere else. [20]

Apparently Twiggs received special orders from the War Department within a day or two of this last appeal to use the camels in an experiment within the Department of Texas. On April 7 he issued Special Order No. 24 "in consequence of instructions from the War Department" to have all available camels at Camp Verde brought to San Antonio. Moreover, he ordered that herders and packers be trained to accompany the animals, who were to be sent into the Big Bend country of southwest Texas.

Major Vinton, the quartermaster at San Antonio, sent orders to Lieutenant Graham, who had charge of the animals, to move them from Camp Verde to the Alamo City. However, only twenty-four were available, the remainder "being young ones and females with young." Vinton reported to General Jesup that inasmuch as this expedition offered the first real test for camels in Texas, he thought it best to use "only those not pregnant nor encumbered with young at their sides." The major problem which Vinton foresaw was that of the drovers employed in the Middle East to care for the animals, only one still remained in Texas; therefore those soldiers going on the expedition needed "a course of instruction in the manner of training and packing the animals for service in the field." [21]

The purpose of the expedition into southwest Texas was to make a topographical survey of the Big Bend region. Commanding the detachment from the Corps of Topographical Engineers assigned to this task was Brevet Second Lieutenant William H. Echols, an officer commissioned less than a year before. In General Twiggs' mind, however, the experiment with camels was sufficiently important that he wanted a more experienced officer there to report; assigned this task was Second Lieutenant Edward L. Hartz. A graduate of West Point, class of 1855, Hartz had been appointed to the Military Academy from his native Pennsylvania, and had been commissioned a second lieutenant in the 7th Infantry the year he completed his education. One month later, in August of 1855, he transferred to the 8th Infantry and was sent to Texas.[22]

Hartz received his instructions from Major Vinton on April 26. These noted that the twenty-four animals, along with six drovers, were commended to his care for the purpose of transporting military supplies and baggage on the projected expedition. Vinton, no doubt with an eye to what General Twiggs wanted on this expedition, as well as to the careful scrutiny which the report of the expedition would receive from high officials in Washington, was careful to note that the camels had been equipped as completely as possible to make the trial a success. Hartz was ordered to report regularly "at intervals no longer than a month" the condition of the animals and the work which they performed. The dromedaries, which at Camp Verde had been fed eight to ten pounds of corn daily, were not to be fed any grain on the trek; rather they were to be encouraged to subsist off native plants and grass along the way. "Still," cautioned Vinton, "they must not lack for anything which may tend to their thorough efficiency."

On the expedition the camels were to be loaded at the beginning with 400 pounds, that weight to be increased "to six hundred pounds as circumstances may warrant—giving the largest camels the heaviest loads." If during the trip the animals had to travel over sloping roads in wet weather, "when the camel, from the peculiar formation of its feet, finds its greatest difficulty in travelling," Hartz was to lighten their burdens by transferring some of what they carried to the mules. And Vinton was sending

Edwart L. Hartz, taken when he was a captain. *Courtesy U. S. Signal Corps (Brady Collection), National Archives.*

along mules, he noted, "as adjuncts, as well as having their ef-ficiency compared with that of the camels as a means of transpor-tation."

To make life as pleasant as possible for the camel drovers, Vin-ton sent "a Wall tent besides certain other articles of Camp Equi-page, and each of them will be provided with a mule." Finally, for Hartz' instruction about dromedaries, he enclosed extracts from various government documents about the animals "from which you may derive some profitable information." [23]

Early in May the twenty-four camels and six drovers left San Antonio bound for Camp Hudson, a post erected on the road to El Paso to protect travelers from marauding Indians. On this journey they accompanied a train of public wagons, easily keeping up with them and arriving at Camp Hudson on May 18; all arrived in good condition except one which somehow sustained a wound on its foot. During the next several days the animals were picketed on the nearby San Pedro River while final preparations were made. During those days Hartz had the animals herded up the slopes of nearby hills to allow them to graze on the grass there, but he noted that "they manifested no particular fondness for these grasses . . . but showed a partiality for browsing upon the leaves of the hackberry, artemisia, wild grape, thistles, and many other plants the names of which are not known to me. . . ." Hartz divided the camels into six trains of four camels each and divided his baggage accordingly. To his disgust, however, the mules provided for the expedition proved "wild and unbroken" and were "not only very difficult to manage, but were even dangerous."

At last on May 23 all was in readiness, the male camels loaded with 500 pounds each, the females with 300 to 400 pounds each. That day the expedition made only a mile and a half, however, for the drovers proved inexperienced and the packs kept shifting and falling. The next day the expedition was delayed by the mules; Hartz noted disgustedly that these hybrids kept trying to get free "in the most frantic manner" of whatever burden was placed on them. During the day Lieutenant Hartz led his party toward the Pecos River through a rough country of broken rocks and ravines. The camels did not keep up as well as the mules because their packs kept shifting, making necessary a constant repacking; Hartz attributed this in part to ignorance on the part of the packers and in part to the good condition of the animals, which had rendered their "humps so full and round that they do not fit into the wedge-shaped cavity of the saddle."

In the days that followed the expedition passed through some of the most rugged country in Texas, country in Hartz' words designed "to test the capabilities of the camel for service": steep hills, out-croppings of rock, river crossings, limestone. Over all this the camels walked with ease and comfort, their feet not bothered at all; Hartz noted that unshod horses and mules would have been lamed. And at camps with little grass the mules had to be picketed some distance away, while the camels patiently ate "almost every bush and herb in the immediate vicinity of the camp." On May 27 and 28 the route was through dry country, and men, horses, and mules were "suffering very much from thirst"; the camels, however, "showed no evidence of fatigue, and did not seem to feel the want of water, which had now become a necessity for the preservation of horses and mules." When at last the expedition reached water on May 29, Hartz was astonished by the indifference with which the camels regarded it—while the mules and horses were almost frantic to drink their fill. Nor were there evidences of saddle sores on the dromedaries' backs, and only one had any chafe marks.

Crossing the Pecos River did prove slightly difficult for the dromedaries, for the banks were a foot or two high and slippery. "One or two camels, failing at first to ascend the bank, became to a certain extent unmanageable, and lay down in the water, wetting their packs, and giving rise to some apprehension for their safety," Hartz reported. However, the drovers found this could be overcome by throwing a little water in their faces, which "brought them to their senses; and, in another effort, they cleared the stream." Here the mules definitely outperformed the camels, for they crossed without any problem.

Next came a mountain with a 30° slope, its sides covered with "irregular masses of rock." Hartz sent the pack mules ahead, hoping they would blaze a trail that could be followed by the camels. However, in the lead train a male dromedary, loaded with more than 500 pounds slipped and fell. He would not get up again until his burden was taken from him. The same happened with the big male leading the second train. Hartz commented that the females, which were more lightly loaded, "seemed better fitted for this work." On the far side the lieutenant made no effort to have the

Gwinn Harris Heap, who was fascinated by wrestling camels, rendered this drawing of an animal trained for this purpose in Asia Minor.

camels carry their loads down to the valley below; men and pack mules accomplished this task.

On June 2, while the column was moving down a narrow trail beside the Pecos, an older camel was shoved from the trail by a younger one. The unfortunate animal "fell down the bank, turning over and over, and but for timely assistance would probably have been lost in the river." One of the drovers leaped into the stream and freed the camel from its load, and it came ashore somewhat lamed by its experience; without a load, it was able to continue the march. The next day on yet another narrow path, a male slipped from a narrow ledge of rock, fell ten or twelve feet with its load, and was "badly sprained in consequence." With its load distributed among the other animals, it also was able to continue the march.

By this time the camels apparently had hardened to life on the trail, and were bearing 400 to 500 pounds each. On June 4 the caravan climbed a mountain with a slope of 22½° "with the greatest ease," just as a crossing of Independence Creek near its juncture with the Pecos was made without incident. Hartz noted that his route that day could not have been traversed by wagons, but that it was "easily practicable for the camels."

Arriving at Fort Lancaster on June 5, Hartz chose to remain there an extra day while his camel master applied various ointments to the chafed backs of several camels, and the mules were allowed to rest. Next the expedition moved on to Comanche Springs. During this journey a camel drover forgot for a moment to keep the males separated, as Hartz had ordered, for the animals were rutting; two of the animals immediately fell to fighting, and before they could be separated one had been bitten severely on the leg, disabling it for several days.

On June 15 Lieutenant Echols, who was technically in command of the entire expedition, sent Hartz "in command of a mounted escort" with twenty camels to make a reconnaissance between Comanche Springs and Independence Creek. Each camel carried slightly more than 350 pounds, under which weight they were able to keep up easily with the horses for twenty-four miles at an average speed of three and one-fourth miles per hour. During the ride the following day the route was impracticable for wagons, but again the camels kept up—and that evening, when Hartz rationed the horses and mules to five quarts of water, the dromedaries he gave none. Arriving at last at Independence Creek on June 17, Hartz noted that the camels "seemed very thirsty" and drank copiously because the weather had been intensely hot; however, the horses and mules, which had received water along the way, "showed signs of failing, and manifested the greatest necessity for water."

On his return to Fort Davis, Hartz noted several times that camels could see as well at night as men and mules, for they traveled after sunset and well into the evening on several occasions without misstep. By June 23 the lieutenant noted that his horses and mules were "showing very evident signs of failing" despite the fact that he had given them water to drink on several occasions; the camels, which had received nothing, were "strong and in good spirits." That day one of the female camels was bitten by a rattlesnake; Hartz directed that the wound be "immediately scarified, some liquid ammonia rubbed in it, and then bound up." That evening, when he examined it, he could find no symptoms to cause any apprehension.

On June 24 the expedition came to Arroyo de las Vacas, a spring full of water. The horses and mules were "nearly famished for want of water"; already some of them were in no condition to be ridden. Yet the camels, which "had borne their burdens from sunrise to nearly sunset . . . had not tasted of the water they carried to sustain the horses and mules. . . . In addition to this, in consequence of the necessity to force the march across this wide waste of waterless country, but little time could be afforded them to feed; notwithstanding these severe trials all of them arrived at the water in good condition, and evinced no evidence of unusual suffering or distress." The distance covered was estimated by a topographical officer at 100 miles. Hartz estimated that an expedition using mules would have had to be extremely large in order to carry the necessary water for men and animals. He concluded, ". . . Not only the capability, but the superiority of the camel for military purposes in the badly-watered sections of country, seems to me to be established." Arriving at Fort Davis on June 26, Hartz found his horses and mules nearly exhausted, his camels strong and vigorous.

From Fort Davis the expedition set out on June 30, each camel carrying approximately 400 pounds. It arrived at Camp Stockton on the El Paso Road on Independence Day, remaining there until July 11 when it departed with twenty-three camels carrying rations for thirty-three days and baggage for fifty men; down the Comanche War Trail they marched for the Rio Grande. In the days that followed, Hartz' report about the camels grew almost monotonous; his entry for July 14 was typical: "The performance of the camels was all that could be desired." Again on July 17 he wrote, "The patience, endurance, and steadiness which characterize the performance of the camels during this march is beyond praise. . . ." On July 19 the objective of reaching the Rio Grande was attained, whereupon they commenced their homeward march. Horses and mules tired, and one had to be abandoned because he could not continue, but the camels continued "lively and contented." At last on August 7 the caravan straggled into Camp Hudson tired, worn, dirty, and severely in need of rest. Hartz ended his diary on notes of fulsome praise for the camel, although he must have known that General Twiggs, commander of the Department of Texas, had little love for the animal.[24]

Hartz' major complaint during this trip into extremely rugged country was that packs kept falling off of the camels. What was needed, he kept suggesting, was better-designed packs and more experienced packers. The only man at Camp Verde who had experience of any length with the animals was Henry Ramsey, who had been employed in the summer of 1857 after Alfred Ray, the original clerk and overseer employed by Major Henry C. Wayne was discharged; this also was after Beale and part of the herd, along with Hi Jolly and Greek George had departed for California; and it was after the Turks and Greeks, who had come to the United States with Wayne or Lieutenant Porter aboard the *Supply*, had voluntarily quit or else had been discharged.

Actually Captain Innis N. Palmer, the commanding officer at Camp Verde when the camels first arrived, had written Secretary of War John B. Floyd on May 20, 1857, wanting to fire the Greeks and Turks who had been employed. Palmer called them "worthless," saying one "is such a disgusting creature in his habits that I do not wish him to remain at the post." His problem was that the contract made with these men in Smyrna or Alexandria called for them to be paid fifty dollars when they were discharged. In addition, two of the Turks wished to be returned to Smyrna at the expense of the United States government as provided in their contract.[25]

By July of 1857 Captain Palmer had discharged all remaining employees brought to the United States by Wayne and Porter. Two of these five men, both Turks from Smyrna, Ali Oglou Suleiman and Mustafa Oglou Hassom, wanted transportation home. Palmer, in his letter to Colonel D. D. Tompkins, the quartermaster at New Orleans, called them "excellent men" and "always faithful," and said the two would be in New Orleans within a week or two. "I hope you will consider yourself authorized to procure transportation for them to Alexandria or Smyrna," Palmer wrote, obviously passing the responsibility along.[26]

Colonel Tompkins was at a loss about his responsibility when Suleiman and Hassom arrived in New Orleans on August 4 and telegraphed Quartermaster General Jesup for instructions.[27] After a complicated series of letters, each bucked up the line to higher authority, Secretary of War John B. Floyd assumed responsibility. Hassom and Suleiman were taken to New York City, arriving there late in August to be quartered at public expense at one dollar per day. On September 12 the two at last boarded the steamer *Vanderbilt* and sailed for Alexandria, Egypt, via Southampton—at a cost to the United States of $325. Once in Southampton, however, the two were unable to board the ship bound for Alexandria, for it was filled with British soldiers bound for India. An agent of the American-European Express and Exchange Company did find them space on the *Australian,* and they departed England for Alexandria on October 12. The American consul at that port, Edwin De Leon, reported on December 4, 1857, that the two had arrived safely; De Leon forwarded a claim for payment of an additional forty-five dollars for their food while there and third-class passage on to Smyrna. De Leon also noted that three Egyptians hired by Wayne and Porter previously had returned to Egypt, and on them he had spent six dollars which he wanted the Army to repay. In all, the return of these drovers to their native lands proved expensive.[28]

Nor was the government through paying. Gwinn Harris Heap, who had ended his connection with the camel experiment when the second shipment of animals arrived in Texas in 1857, received a letter in November 1859 from California in which he was asked to secure back pay for Hi Jolly and Greek George. Heap forwarded these letters to Major Ebenezer S. Sibley at the Quartermaster Office of the Army, requesting that the men receive what was due them. Quartermaster General Jesup on January 17, 1860, wrote Lieutenant Davidson at Fort Tejon, authorizing him to pay any back wages due, plus the fifty dollars in separation pay.[29]

All foreign employment on the project thus had come to an end, although Hi Jolly would continue as a civilian employee in California for months to come. In California the herd was quartered at Fort Tejon, Fort Yuma, and Los Angeles, with a few at the port city of San Pedro. In Texas the animals had returned to Camp Verde where Henry Ramsey occasionally took a few to San Antonio for forage. By the fall of 1860 the only excitement connected with the project was the question of castrating some of the males at Camp Verde to see if this would reduce their fighting instincts during the rutting season. Major Vinton agreed that two of the males should be thus "altered," and, if this operation was performed successfully, then the remainder, except two needed for stud purposes, might similarly be operated on.[30]

Apparently Secretary of War John B. Floyd was not discouraged by the return of the Greeks and Turks, for he remained enthusiastic about the capabilities of the camels. In his annual report to the President in December 1859 he wrote that the experiments, "and they are pretty full," with the animals constituted "a most useful and economical means of transportation for men and supplies through the great deserts and barren regions of our interior." Camels, he asserted, could carry burdens across terrain so rough and precipitous that mules could scarcely cross it unloaded and could do so without carrying large supplies of water. "As a measure of economy and efficiency, I cannot too strongly recommend the purchase of a full supply to the favorable consideration of Congress," he concluded.[31] By December 1860, when Floyd made his last annual report, he made no mention of the Camel Corps, for national events had superseded this experiment.

While the camels in Texas and California grazed contentedly, their lives in tune with the natural rhythms which governed them, the citizens of the United States had no such natural rhythm to govern their political affairs. That autumn of 1860, passion replaced reason as the national elections came, bringing Abraham Lincoln to the Presidency—and secession to the nation. Lincoln once stated that the nation could not endure "half slave, half free." Certainly during the war that followed, an army fighting for national survival—or to establish national sovereignty in the South—could not afford experiments with camels. The Camel Corps had to be disbanded and the animals sold.

7 SALE OF THE HERD

On December 20, 1860, as the Lone Star State drifted rapidly toward secession, Brevet Major General David E. Twiggs, Federal commander for the Department of Texas, paused amidst his troubles to recommend one last time that the camels at Camp Verde be sold. This he urged on the score of retrenchment, suggesting that the animals be disposed of at public auction " *for what they will bring"*; if no one submitted a bid, then he wanted them "turned *loose on the prairie and abandoned."* This move, he asserted, would save the government the $560 per month then being spent on their upkeep.[1]

Less than two weeks later, on January 2, 1861, he was writing to his superiors in Washington asking what disposition to make of government property should Texas secede. Again on January 15 he wrote, this time to Commanding General of the Army Winfield Scott that the situation in Texas was growing critical and asking for instructions. By then it was too late, for state officials were already moving to take charge of all Federal stores, weapons, and supplies—even animals—for the Confederacy, and

Georgia-born David E. Twiggs made no real effort to oppose this. Too late the secretary of war realized what was transpiring; on January 28, the same day the Texas secession convention met, John B. Floyd ordered Twiggs relieved from command at San Antonio. Camp Verde fell into Confederate hands on February 28, 1861, the officer taking charge noting that at the post were "eighty camels." The only use for the beasts which came to the minds of the captors was as entertainment for some of the local ladies and children who were given rides.

J. W. Walker, a lad of fifteen who joined a Texas Ranger company at Camp Verde in 1862, was assigned to herd the animals. He stayed with them for more than a year, during which time some of the animals were used to pack salt found near Brownsville to San Antonio, as well as salt from San Elizario (near El Paso) to San Antonio; this salt eventually was sent east to help other Confederate states with no supply of their own. The Texans assigned to duty, most of them young lads like Walker, hated the animals intensely and mistreated them. One later confessed that when one camel refused to keep up with the others, he grew angry at the animal and killed it with his knife. In 1863 three of the animals somehow were allowed to wander off from the herd. Incredibly, these three dromedaries in the midst of war managed to make their way to Arkansas where they were "captured" by Federal troops. For safekeeping the animals were sent to Iowa to the custody of a "Mr. Paden" who had property on the Des Moines River. A young assistant Quartermaster officer in the Department of Missouri, Lieutenant J. Gaylee, wrote to his commanding general, John M. Schofield, to ask what disposition should be made of the three beasts. Schofield replied on July 1, 1863, that the camels should be taken to St. Louis for sale at auction "after proper advertisement a reasonable time." [2]

The Confederates never figured out any proper use for the camels. Some were given to the Postal Service for a time and used to deliver mail in rural areas around San Antonio. Another was used by General Sterling Price throughout the war to transport his personal baggage, while some were used to transport cotton to Mexico, one bale on each side of the animals to balance them.

One camel was pushed over a bluff by Confederate soldiers who thought the animal was too much trouble to look after; the fall broke the animal's neck, killing it instantly. Thereafter the spot was known as "Camel's Leap." J. W. Walker summed up the Confederate attitude toward the animals when he commented, "They were like a wart on a stick. We had them and couldn't get rid of them."

At last the war dragged to a close, and on June 19, 1865, Federal troops came ashore at Galveston to proclaim Texas back in the Union—and say that all Confederate property was confiscated. At that point Henry Ramsey, who had been hired by officers at Camp Verde in 1858 as overseer of the camels, suddenly remembered his responsibility and wrote the new commanding general in Texas: "I have at Camp Verde 66 Camels property of the United States in my possession." Not only did he want to report this Federal property, but also he wanted to be paid for the money "I necessarily expended in caring for them." [3]

The matter of the camels was referred to Colonel E. G. Sawtelle, the quartermaster at New Orleans, headquarters for the Military Division of the Gulf. Sawtelle, in turn, passed the matter to the quartermaster general "for instructions." The quartermaster general likewise chose to duck the issue by referring it to Secretary of War Edwin M. Stanton, writing, "While I have no doubt that in hands interested in them, they could be made useful in the inland trade of the central & desert regions of the continent, I cannot ascertain that these have ever been so employed as to be of any advantage to the Military Service, and I do not think that it will be practicable to make them useful." However, wrote the quartermaster general, the sale of the animals would put them into private hands where they might be used for profit—and the benefit of the country.

Secretary of War Stanton concurred with this recommendation, and the animals in Texas were ordered sold at public bid in New Orleans. Sawtelle accordingly advertised the sixty-six dromedaries for sale, and on March 7, 1866, opened the bids at New Orleans. To his dismay the highest bid was thirty-one dollars per animal. That evening at 7:40 p.m. he wired Quartermaster General M. C. Meigs, "Shall I sell them at that price?" The answer was explicit: "Let the camels be sold at the highest bid offered." When Colonel Sawtelle finally turned in his report of the bidding, it showed that only three men, all from San Antonio, Texas, had submitted bids: Bethel Coopwood at thirty-one dollars each; Joseph Hallam at ten dollars each; and Horace Bell, who wanted to pay twenty-five dollars for just four of the animals or five dollars each for all sixty-six animals. Coopwood's bid was accepted.[4]

Bethel Coopwood was a man of interesting background. Born in 1827 in Alabama, he immigrated to Texas in 1846 where he immediately joined the Army to fight in the Mexican War. Then in 1854 he moved to California and was admitted to the bar as an attorney, then returned to Texas where he settled in the Rio Grande Valley to practice law—and raise a family of fourteen children. During the Civil War he served the Confederacy as a captain of cavalry until his discharge in 1863 because of a wound he had received in a courtroom brawl years earlier.[5] At one time he had been a Mormon, but by 1865 he had renounced that religion.

The proud owner of sixty-six camels in March 1866, Coopwood immediately sold five of them to Ringling Brothers Circus reportedly for $3745. Inasmuch as he had paid only $2046 for the entire lot, he already had made a handsome profit. The rest he drove to Laredo to begin an overland packing service between that Texas border town and Mexico City. However, this business failed, as Coopwood lamented later, because of "thieving Mexicans and desperate white men." Some of the animals he sold to circus owners in Mexico, others to anyone expressing an interest in owning one of them. For years these former Army camels were exhibited in Mexico. Later, when Coopwood brought his remaining stock across the border into the United States once again, the Army apparently decided the animals were government property, for they still bore the government's brand. Coopwood apparently had lost interest, for he did not press his suit to ownership until the government had become disillusioned and released the animals. Reportedly the herd was last seen traveling west toward

Arizona. Coopwood then brought suit against the government for damages, but during his lifetime he could never get reimbursed by Congress. Thus ended the Texas herd.[6]

The animals in California fared only slightly better. At the outbreak of the Civil War some of the animals were at Fort Yuma, others at Fort Mohave, and yet others at San Pedro. Apparently these were moved about within the Department from time to time, for on August 25, 1862, a civilian named R. M. Stockton wrote the commanding officer at Camp Latham, California, to propose that "all the Camels now in possession of your Quarter Master at Camp Latham" be turned over to him until the government should want them back. In return he would breed them "as rapidly as their nature will permit" and work them for profit, also keeping for himself a part of the increase.[7]

Another person in California interested in the camels was Edward Fitzgerald Beale. He likewise wanted to take the government herd to keep; he promised to pasture the herd at his El Tejon Ranch, returning to the government all their natural increase in numbers. Major E. B. Babbitt, a Quartermaster officer, suggested to Colonel R. C. Drum, assistant adjutant general for California, that the animals should not be given over to either man, but rather should be offered for sale: ". . . These animals have rendered no service for two years, and are not likely to do so." [8]

Actually one last major test came for the camels in California. In January of 1863 the animals were used to carry the mail and Army dispatches across the desert from Los Angeles to Tucson, but this ended quickly; the men assigned to make the ride came to hate the animals bitterly.[9] That same year on May 21, 1863, Major Clarence Bennett wrote from Camp Drum, California, to Colonel R. C. Drum that at his post there were thirty-six camels performing no useful service, that they were being fed on government forage, and that the men assigned to care for them bitterly hated the beasts. Bennett's recommendation was to use the animals to haul mail and dispatches between the various Army posts in the state and to Tucson, Arizona.[10] His request was denied.

Lieutenant Colonel Babbitt, the deputy quartermaster general for California, apparently decided from all this correspondence that the camels served no real function and should be sold in order to reduce expenses. On August 1, 1863, he wrote General Meigs, commanding general of the Department, to recommend their sale: "It is with reluctance that I have been induced to commend the public sale of the camels, which were brought to our shores with so much care and expense and with high hopes of their great utility, but in view of the fact that for years they have been but a constant source of expense to the Govt. without the slightest return in the way of service; I cannot do less [than recommend] . . . they might be sold at San Francisco at a fair price." [11] An endorsement on the cover of Babbitt's letter from Colonel Drum stated, "Approved and respectfully submitted." From Meigs the recommendation went to Washington where the quartermaster general and then the secretary of war gave their approval. On September 9, 1863, the order was given that the animals in California were to be sold at public auction.

To all the posts in California where camels were stabled, the order went early in November to transport the animals to Benecia Barracks (north of San Francisco). The herd from San Pedro proceeded north along the coast, causing a sensation in villages along the way. Horses snorted and shied, throwing costumed vaqueros, while cattle stampeded at the smell. The San Francisco *Daily Evening Bulletin* of January 8, 1864, carried a story reprinted from Santa Barbara that camels had passed through the town herded by six men and that "Ranchero hands run wild with fear when they see them." Captain William G. Morris, who brought one of the herds, reported on November 19 to Colonel Babbitt that the animals he had in his charge were "in first rate condition." [12]

A total of thirty-six camels were brought to Benecia Barracks, and on February 26, 1864, they were sold at auction for the sum of $1945, less a 2½ per cent commission. Nevertheless, Colonel Babbitt was pleased, writing General Meigs, "The amount of sale was less than I had hoped for, but when I consider that they were absolutely unserviceable for any Government purpose, I cannot but regard their sale at even a less price as a decided benefit to the

U. States." [13] The purchaser was Samuel McLaughlin, [14] who thought to use the animals to pack freight to Nevada, then a booming mining camp. Almost immediately, however, he sold three to a rancher named Riley for use in Wilson's Circus. Riley drove the animals to a nearby pasture for safekeeping, but immediately had difficulty. In the pasture with them were some mules—at least, there were mules in the pasture the evening the camels were put in it. The next morning the mules were gone, frightened by the strange smell. And teams of horses and mules driving on a road beside the pasture bolted and ran away when they saw and smelled the newcomers. Riley was told to move the animals at once. [15]

McLaughlin, meanwhile, had taken the remainder of his newly purchased dromedaries to his ranch in Sonoma County. Shortly thereafter he selected ten of the animals with which to begin his freight line to Nevada. On his way to start that enterprise he passed through Sacramento; there he discovered the state fair in progress and thought he might make some easy money by placing the animals on exhibit and by staging a race. A newspaper reporter who examined the herd stated that seven of the ten were native born, ranging in age from two to four years. However, in the herd was "Old Tule," no doubt the same dromedary noted on the Beale expedition, for his age was estimated at thirty-five. The "Great Dromedary Race" proved to be a fiasco, for the riders found the peculiar rocking gate of a camel disconcerting and completed the race on muleback, but the gate receipt was $180, indicating that at least 360 people paid the fifty-cent admission fee. [16]

McLaughlin, disappointed at the small profit he had made, started for Nevada, but paused at Marysville to stage yet another dromedary race. Afterward he returned to Sacramento, sending the animals on to the Comstock Lode country of Nevada under the care of Greenhood and Company, each camel packing a 400-pound load. The arrival of this caravan did not please the teamsters in and around Comstock, for their horses and mules bolted in fright when they saw the strange newcomers. McLaughlin was warned several times to remove the camels from that vicinity, and

"Drove of Bactrian Camels, en route for Washoe by the Bigtree Route, passing through the Mammoth Grove, Sept. 1860," by Edward Vischer. *Courtesy California Section, California State Library.*

a few sniping shots at his animals made the warnings have extra meaning. McLaughlin then used the beasts for a chore no one else seemed eager to perform: transporting salt the 200 miles from a marsh in Esmeralda County, Nevada, to the Washoe crushing mill (salt was needed in crushing the ore to extract the silver). A professor from Yale University, visiting the area in 1865, stated that he examined the camels involved in this task; he wrote, "Their backs had not been cared for, and they had been used in packing heavy loads of salt from the deserts. Salt Water and alkali had accumulated in the long hair of their humps, their pack saddles had galled them, and great loathsome sores nearly covered the parts touched by the saddle." [17]

When salt was discovered closer to the mines, putting McLaughlin out of this business, he decided to move the animals to Fort Yuma, Arizona, where he thought they might find a buyer. Going with him on this trek were two of his drovers, Hi Jolly and Greek George. Just as the caravan reached Yuma, however, McLaughlin died, and the two immigrants decided to turn the camels loose at that place.

The thirty-six camels sold at Benecia Barracks in 1864 did not constitute all the government's dromedaries in California. The rest were sold at various places, some bought by circus owners, a few by enterprising tavern owners who stabled the animals behind their establishments to be viewed for purchasing drinks, and yet others ending up in zoos. Edward Fitzgerald Beale managed to buy several of the animals and take them to his El Tejon ranch, which he owned in partnership with S. A. Bishop. There he kept them until the herd died a natural death, using them to construct roads and making trips. In fact, he trained two of the animals to pull a sulky, and in this he would ride the 100 miles to Los Angeles; reportedly he talked to the animals "in Syrian which he had with characteristic energy taught himself for this purpose." [18]

In Nevada the animals imported by Otto Esche and sold to Julius Bandmann and others also were employed in transporting salt and in various freighting enterprises. There the animals remained for years, some used by a mining company on one occasion to carry wood to the top of 9000-foot Mount Davidson

"Lake near the Summit of East Range, on the Big Tree Route," by Edward Vischer, which shows the camels being driven to Nevada. *Courtesy California Section, California State Library.*

near Virginia City, each animal carrying one-third of a cord each trip; this wood was used to make a huge bonfire atop the mountain on July 4, 1876, the centennial of American independence. Reportedly this fire could be seen "from all parts of the Washoe Valley and other places within a radius of many miles." [19]

As the animals in Nevada gradually wore out from hard service and misuse, they were turned loose to forage in their old age. There they probably were joined by some of the camels which had been used in British Columbia and then abandoned to wander south. The great shaggy animals naturally scared the horses and mules of farmers, creating such a nuisance that Hugh Carling of Lyon County introduced legislation in the state legislature on January 19, 1875, entitled, "An Act to prohibit camels and dromedaries from running at large on or about the public highways of the State of Nevada." Owners of such animals thereby were prohibited from allowing camels to run at large on public roads; the fine for this offense was a fine of "not less than twenty-five (25); or more than one hundred (100) dollars, or by imprisonment not less than ten or more than thirty days, or by both such fine and imprisonment." This act was not repealed until 1899.[20]

Some of the camels in Nevada did not fare so badly, however. A Frenchman who owned a ranch on the Carson River apparently took pity on the mistreated animals he saw and bought or rounded up several of them.[21] Local rumor held that the Frenchman at one time had served with the French Army in Algeria, and there had come to have an affection for camels; perhaps, some said, his life had been saved by one of the beasts. At his ranch these animals fattened, and there they increased until the herd numbered thirty-six. The patriarch of this herd was a great animal named "Old Heenan," [22] a giant with hair on parts of his body from twelve to eighteen inches long.

Mexican employees on a nearby ranch owned by Sam Buckland believed that this hair, if carded and spun, could be woven into a rope of exceptional quality. One day two of these Mexicans, Antonio and Gedonio, took sheep shears and a rope and set out to shear Old Heenan, unaware of the fact that the camel was

"Descent to Carson Valley," by Edward Vischer; this scene depicts the taking of camels to Nevada in 1875. *Courtesy California Section, California State Library.*

The civilian camel express between Virginia City and Austin, Nevada, in 1875. *Courtesy U. S. Bureau of Public Roads, National Archives.*

in rutting season. They found him guarding his harem while contentedly munching on greasewood plants. Fearing that their mustang ponies would rear in fright at smell of the camels, Gedonio dismounted and approached Old Heenan on foot. The dromedary stood still, patiently chewing and watching through half-closed eyes. Gedonio cast his lasso true and began to pull the animal toward him.

Suddenly the beast became aware of what was happening, and there no longer was need for Gedonio to pull on the rope. Old

Heenan, his eyes filled with rage, was charging toward him, hissing and screeching. The Mexican thought for a moment that the rope would choke the animal into submission, but as the huge beast charged still faster he decided that Old Heenan might be able to live as long without air as without water; moreover, the animal was charging so fast there was no way to pull properly on the rope and cut off his supply of air. Gedonio thereupon threw down the rope and ran for his life.

For a time the fleeing Mexcian was able to dodge among the greasewood, but these were only two or three feet high and afforded little protection. Gedonio at last decided his only safety lay in the nearby river and ran for that, thinking to climb to safety in a cottonwood tree. However, when he arrived at the stream, the camel was so close that Gedonio jumped into the river. Unable to swim, he moved out in the stream until the water was up to his neck. Heenan, close behind, fortunately did not feel like a swim and stood on the bank spitting his cud on the face of the yelling Mexican.

Antonio, who on horseback had watched his partner's inglorious flight, could not see below the riverbank and feared at first that Gedonio had been drowned. Approaching the river, he shouted until Gedonio replied, explaining how the situation stood—and begging for help. He suggested that Antonio should tie the two horses together, then approach on foot, grab the rope trailing from Heenan's neck, and tie this securely around a cottonwood tree. Antonio did as suggested, but when he attempted to tie the rope around the tree he found it short by a foot or two—and his tugging on it attracted the attention of Old Heenan who turned and, with teeth bared, came toward him. Antonio fled up the bank, intending to climb aboard his horse and ride to safety, but at sight of the camel the two mustangs, tied together, snorted and ran. Heenan turned his attention to these two animals and pursued them, leaving the two Mexicans alive but afoot.

Gedonio climbed from the river while Antonio pulled himself from the clump of sagebrush into which he had dived for safety, and the two set out in search of their horses. Half a mile away they found Old Heenan standing guard over a deep hole in the river into which the two horses had plunged—and drowned. The two Mexicans waited until Heenan grew tired of his vigil and wandered back to his harem, after which with great difficulty they managed to unfasten their saddles and bridles from the dead horses and walk back to the ranch. Not only had they failed to get wool for a camelhair rope, but also they had lost their horses—as well as their sheep shears.

That evening in the bunkhouse the two Mexicans told a long fabricated story about how they had come to lose their horses, but unfortunately for them the Frenchman who owned the camels had observed the entire episode. When he told the true story, there was great merriment at the expense of Antonio and Gedonio, their employer, Sam Buckland, leading in the laughter. After a week of hearing their mistake in trying to shear a male camel in rutting season, the two Mexicans quietly disappeared one night, two of Buckland's horses leaving with them. Thereafter Buckland found little amusement in this story.[23]

Another encounter with the camels, this time in Arizona, ended in similar embarrassment. This one involved a German miner who loved to hunt and who, every weekend, loaded his rifle and went into the hills, returning with wild stories about the huge animals he had wounded. One Sunday he came tearing into camp shouting, "Poys, I half shooted a hel-ak."

"A what?" someone asked.

"A hel-ak, a hel-ick!" he replied. "Mine Gott, es war de biggerest hel-ak das in all dese mountains sall wohnen. . . . She was a frau hel-ak, she vas der grandmother of all der hel-aks in the vorldt!"

Another German in the crowd, one with a better command of English, translated for Hans, informing the miners that a hel-ak was an elk. When some of them expressed disbelief in Hans' story, he showed them blood on his knife and even his rifle. As the camp needed fresh meat, two miners took horses and set out with Hans, who bragged that the animal would yield "a vagonload" of meat. During the ride to where the carcass lay, Hans admitted that he never before had seen an elk, but he had heard everyone in camp speak of them and thought he recognized the one he had shot from the description given him. Arriving at the spot, the two miners looked at the animal, at first having difficulty identifying it because Hans, in his excitement to make certain it was dead, had almost cut its head off.

At last came recognition. "By the holy poker," exclaimed one, "he has killed one of the camels that belong over at the other camp!" Seeing Hans' consternation and a chance to have some fun, he continued, "I have no doubt the animal is worth all of a thousand dollars."

Hans missed the joke at first. Rather his excitement increased, for he explained that he had seen a whole herd of the animals nearby. "Ah, Gott," he exclaimed, "if we could only kill dem all it is more as twenty thousand dollar in our pocket!"

When at last the two explained to Hans that it was he who would have to pay the thousand dollars, not receive it, he grew fearful, and all three left the scene as quickly as possible. Back at the camp all the miners enjoyed a great laugh about the "elk" which Hans had killed. For several days Hans endured the laughter, the story growing to the point where everyone agreed that the animal was worth at least $1500. At last Hans could stand it no more and slipped away from the camp.

He was not to escape so easily, however. Five months later a miner from the camp where the camel had been shot moved to a new job a hundred miles away to accept employment. That same day when a meal was served and all hands were gathered, he recognized the German hunter. "Well, by the holy poker!" he shouted, "here is Hans! Here is the man who shot the camel." Of course, everyone there wanted to hear the story—everyone except Hans who that night slunk away from the place.[24]

The camels owned and employed in various companies in Arizona and Nevada gradually were turned loose in their old age to fend for themselves. Possibly they joined the strays loosed at Fort Yuma or in Texas or from Nevada or even from far-off British Columbia. The last known survivor of the animals originally brought from the Middle East by Major Henry C. Wayne and Lieutenant David D. Porter, along with their descendants, was Old Topsy. The *Oakland Tribune* of April 27, 1934, noted the death of this animal:

Los Angeles.—Topsy, the last camel that trekked across the desert of Arizona and California is dead. Attendants at Griffith Park here destroyed her after she became crippled with paralysis in the park lot where she spent the declining years of her life.

Topsy was the last survivor of the camel herds that once carried packs across the mountains and lava beds of Arizona and Southern California. They were imported on orders of Jefferson Davis, then Secretary of War, as agents of transportation in the desert regions. When their need disappeared, most of the camels were abandoned to live in a wild state on the Arizona desert. Some of the survivors were later captured and sent to zoos, and among them was Topsy.

Of the drovers imported from the Middle East by Wayne and Porter to care for the animals, only two achieved any real fame in the West, Greek George and Hi Jolly. Greek George, according to one report, killed a man in New Mexico about 1866 and was found dead later in the countryside; this story held that he committed suicide rather than be captured and stand trial.[25] Better records exist to indicate that Greek George returned to California where in 1867 he was naturalized an American citizen with the name George Allen. In Los Angeles he lived in a modest adobe house near the present Santa Monica Boulevard in Hollywood. There in 1903 he was visited by Charles F. Lummis who described Greek George as "a modest, well-mannered, sturdy man, with a Homeric beard and a thatch of hair, both so dense as to seem bullet proof." Lummis asserted that in the half century since George had departed Smyrna he had forgotten his Greek and had learned no English; however, he did speak "Spanish, and that very well, after the California models." He died at Mission Viejo near Montebello, California, on September 2, 1913, and was buried at Whittier.[26]

Hi Jolly did not live so long, but his later life was slightly more colorful. Born Hadji Ali in Syria in 1828, he had come to the United States with Porter and the second load of camels early in 1857 because he dreamed of finding a fortune in gold; apparently stories of the mineral wealth of California had reached his native land. Once in Texas he at first was discouraged, but after Beale departed with the camels to survey the 35th parallel road to California he hurried after the expedition to reach the land of his

Photo of Hadji Ali (Hi Jolly) and his bride, taken in Tucson at the time of his wedding. *From the Arizona Historical Society.*

dreams. At Fort Tejon he had been discouraged to learn that he still was a long way from the mines and had continued to work with the camels at Fort Tejon, crossing the desert many times. Still later he went to Nevada for the same reason, for that was where mining was taking place. He never was able to turn dream into reality, however, and after turning the camels loose at Fort Yuma in 1865, he accepted employment with the soldiers moving to Arizona to reopen the posts there after the end of the Civil War.

From Camp McDowell, Arizona Territory, he addressed a letter to General John M. Schofield on July 3, 1870, stating that because of a recent order of the Quartermaster Department to discharge many civilian employees he had been left unemployed. He noted the circumstances that had brought him to the United States, and argued that his original contract guaranteed him "continual employment from the U.S. government as long as my conduct entitles me to such a benefit." Therefore he asked either for another job or else payment of his return passage to his home. Captain George R. Lunford of Camp McDowell endorsed this letter, stating, "Hadji Ali has been a faithful servant of the government for many years. Every officer who has known him speaks well of him, and I believe his services to be valuable to the government." Unfortunately for Hi Jolly, his original contract did not make such provisions as he recalled in 1870.[27]

Apparently he found new employment with the government, however, for he was working for the Army at Tucson in 1880 when he finally was naturalized an American citizen with the name Philip Tedro. General George Crook used him as a packer during the Geronimo campaign of 1885–86. During his work in southern Arizona he met, wooed, and married Gertrude Serna of Tucson, and to them two daughters, Amelia and Herminia, were born. A description of him at this time said he was "short, stocky, dark, with a large, bulbous nose. He had a friendly disposition and spoke very broken English. His Spanish was much better."

In 1889 domestic tranquility grew tiresome, and Hi Jolly set out to make his fortune at last from prospecting. During his packing experiences with the Army, he had traversed the Plomasa, the Harcuvar, and Harqua Halla Mountains between Wickenburg and Quartzsite, and to this area he went, living in a cabin near Quartzsite, Arizona (about eighty miles north of Yuma Crossing). Reportedly he would capture a wild camel from time to time, using the animal on his prospecting trips. At other times he was reported selling water from casks carried on camelback along lonely and dry stretches of roads in the region. Nine years later, in 1898, he tired of prospecting and returned to Tucson to seek forgiveness from his wife, but she and her parents, who were raising the two little girls, refused to take him in. Hi Jolly therefore returned to Quartzsite to live the years he had remaining. Friends in the area tried to secure him a pension from the Army, but during his many years of service he had never enlisted formally and was ineligible for any benefits. Thus his last years were spent in poverty, living off the kindness of ranchers and prospectors. He died at Quartzsite on December 16, 1902. Marking his grave was a modest wooden headboard, as was customary in that area, but in 1935 the Arizona Highway Department recognized his unique contributions to the region by erecting over his remains a pyramidal tombstone topped with a metal camel.[28]

The Hi Jolly Monument in Arizona. *From the Arizona Historical Society.*

A third drover who came to the United States influenced the course of history, but in Mexico, not the United States. A Turk named Elías, he had moved from Texas into New Mexico by the 1860s, but then moved south of the border into Sonora, there to marry a Yaqui Indian girl, operate a ranch, and raise a family. One of the children of that marriage was Plutarcho Elías Calles, who would be president of Mexico from 1924 to 1928; as a youngster he was known as *El Turco*, and even when president he recalled his father speak of herding camels for the United States Army in the American Southwest.[29]

The use of camels by the government and by private industry thus came to a close sometime in the 1870s. The only formal occasions associated with the end of the experiment were the two auctions conducted by the Army, one in California in 1864, the other at New Orleans in 1866. Animals for which the government had paid an average of $250 each, plus transportation, went for fifty dollars in one case, thirty-one dollars in the other. In addition to the government's efforts to use the animals for military purposes, various companies and individuals had tried in vain to make a profit from the labor of the dromedary, but always the hostility of horses and mules, to say nothing of teamsters and packers, had frustrated these plans. Few people seemed willing to accept the camel as anything other than a curiosity, as, for example, the desired use of the animal by the Horrible Club of Virginia City, Nevada, late in June of 1876. This was an organization that prided itself on two points: patriotic pageantry and grotesque performances. As July 4, 1876, approached, the centennial of American independence, members of this club approached the Board of Aldermen in the city to ask for $1000 to aid in securing and decorating a herd of camels for use in an Independence Day parade. At first the aldermen approved the project, but then they had second thoughts and vetoed it; the reason was that they remembered how dromedaries scared horses and mules, and they did not want to ruin the big celebration planned in their city.[30]

Perhaps the Horrible Club of Virginia City was correct in seeing the camel as something both patriotic and grotesque. Certainly the animal had been a pioneer in the American West, but also it repelled most citizens of that area.

Yet the camel did not disappear from the United States when it was turned loose in the deserts of the West. For three-quarters of a century and more, stories would circulate about wild camels having been sighted. Its former owners might want to be rid of it, but the dromedary did not disappear so easily.

8
THE
ENDURING
LEGEND
OF THE
CAMEL

The dromedaries turned loose by the Army or by their corporate or individual owners were more fortunate than their brothers and sisters kept by circus owners and tavern operators. In the era immediately after the Civil War, there were no associations to prevent cruelty to animals, and many of them were cruelly mistreated. Yet the animals running wild were incapable of understanding their advantage—and, had they been able to understand, they could have made a convincing argument that they too were suffering.

Indians who came upon one of these newly emancipated beasts tried to kill them for food. Cowboys and prospectors usually took handgun or rifle and fired at any they saw, while teamsters were most eager to exterminate this source of fright to their own animals. On some occasions one of the camels was recaptured and put to work once again, or else put to more bizarre use, as was the case of "The Red Ghost," an animal whose strange hauntings can be traced in the pages of the Kingman, Arizona, *Mohave County Miner.*

The first notice of this animal came in the spring of 1883. At a lonely adobe house beside Eagle Creek in southeastern Arizona, two women and their children had been left alone when their men went to see about some sheep reportedly killed or stolen by Geronimo and his Apache warriors. During the morning one of the women went to fetch a bucket of water from a spring hidden nearby by willow trees. Dogs were prized by these people as lookouts for Indians, and one in the yard at this house suddenly began to bark so ferociously that the other woman ran to a window and looked to see what had stirred the animal. She heard the woman outside screaming, but she did not rush out to the rescue for she saw something huge and red, seemingly ridden by a man—or devil. The woman inside barricaded the door and stayed inside praying earnestly until the men returned.

That night the men returned and, hearing the story, went outside with torches to search. They found the other woman dead near the spring, and in the mud were cloven hoofprints twice as large as those of a horse. On the willows they found long, red hairs. A coroner was brought from Solomonville. At first he thought the family members must have killed the woman, refusing to believe the hysterical tale of the surviving wife; however, the severely trampled body and the hoofprints in the mud convinced him that the deceased had met "death in some manner unknown."

A few days later and several miles to the northeast, two prospectors panning along Chase's Creek were awakened when their tent came crashing down on them. More frightening yet were the loud screams they heard along with thundering hoofs. Climbing from under the debris of their tent, they saw in the moonlight a very large animal moving rapidly away. They rushed to the nearby town of Ore where they told their story, and several miners returned to search the scene with them. In the mud along the creek they found huge footprints, and on the bushes leading away from the ruined tent they found long, red hair.

Soon stories were circulating about a Red Ghost. Westerners loved a tall tale, and some raconteurs embellished the few known facts about this giant beast. One man claimed he had pursued the animal only to have it vanish before his eyes, while another told of seeing the animal kill and eat a grizzly bear. A month later Cyrus Hamblin, a rancher near the Salt River, went hunting stray cattle when suddenly across a ravine he saw a large red animal. In recounting the story Hamblin declared that the sight of the animal caused the hair to rise on the back of his neck, but he remained as the beast moved out into the open a quarter of a mile away. Suddenly he recognized the animal as a camel—and saw that tied to its back was something which resembled a man, but not one that was alive.

Hamblin was widely known as a man of truth, but still the scoffers laughed. What he had seen was merely the camel's hump, they said. Then several weeks later and sixty miles away, five prospectors saw the same thing. Near the Verde River they came upon the camel with something on its back; they crept closer to get within shooting range, whereupon they opened fire. However, they apparently missed, for the animal was last seen running away rapidly. During the camel's dash for life, the burden on its back fell off. Naturally the prospectors hurried to see what prize they had won. It turned out to be "a human skull with a few shreds of flesh and hair still clinging to it."

This bit of physical evidence, when brought into Kingman, convinced even the skeptics that a huge red camel was running loose with the rest of a corpse tied to its back. Most concluded that some weary pilgrim, faint from thirst, had tied himself to the animal so it would take him to water, only he died before the camel felt the need for a drink. Unable to free itself from this burden, the dromedary retaliated by attacking all humans.

A few days after the prospectors shot at this camel—he was no longer considered an apparition—a freighter and his helpers decided to halt for the night on the banks of the Verde River a few miles to the north. On the wagons were several kegs of whiskey; skeptics later could charge that their story was colored by their drinking some of what was on the wagons. Their version was that after they bedded down for the night, they suddenly were awakened by a loud scream, after which a giant beast at least thirty-feet tall landed in their midst. This alone, they said, knocked over two of the wagons. The teamster, his helpers, and his mules fled into the night to remain hidden until daylight—and perhaps sobriety—revealed to them the source of their trouble. The next morning, when they found sufficient courage to return to camp, all they found were cloven hoofprints and red hair clinging to the side on one overturned wagon.

Almost a year later a cowboy working east of Phoenix on the Anchor-JOT ranch came riding up to a branding corral which, at that time of year, should have been empty. However, inside the corral was a strange animal eating the grass that had grown there. The cowboy had his lasso in hand, and as the huge animal came charging out he roped it. Only then did he realize that the beast was a camel, one headed straight for him and his horse. The horse reared and turned, as it normally would have done to escape a charging bull, but the camel did not keep charging by as a steer would have done; instead it hit horse and rider, knocking them to the ground, and then kept going. During all this the cowboy managed to notice that on the camel's back were the remains of a man.

In the years that followed, stories about the Red Ghost grew in number, although the body tied to it had apparently come apart and fell off. Perhaps then the great camel became less vindictive toward humans and ceased its attacks, for no other stories surfaced about unprovoked rampages by the Red Ghost.

Nine years later Mizoo Hastings of Ore, Arizona, a rancher on the San Francisco River, awakened one morning to notice out his window that a huge red camel was eating his turnip garden. Hastings grabbed his rifle, steadied his aim on the window sill, and killed the Red Ghost. Everyone was convinced such was the case, for on the body was a patchwork of knotted rawhide strips, some of which had been on him so long that "strands had cut their way into the flesh," according to the *Mohave County Miner* of February 25, 1893. An examination of the knots showed that they could not have been tied by the rider of so many years; the corpse had not once been a thirsty man trying to stay on the camel until he went to water. "The only question is whether the man was tied on him for revenge," asked the *Miner*, "or merely as an ugly piece of humor by someone who had a camel and a corpse for which he had no use." [1]

Such tales persisted. Sometimes the person seeing the animal was a cowboy, at others a prospector; soldiers and travelers likewise on occasion swore to having viewed wandering dromedaries. The reports came from the Gila Valley, from the mountains of northern Arizona, from Mexico, from Nevada, even from Utah and southern California. Sometimes the animals were reported singly, other times in large herds. Most such stories, when they appeared in the newspapers, were followed by an editor's comment about the person having had too much to drink or being out in the sun too long, but on occasion there were sightings by persons of such reputation that their stories could not be discounted.

For example, the United States and Mexico in 1901 sent a joint boundary commission to run and mark the line dividing the two nations. Officers attached to this project reported seeing wild camels in southern Arizona; they said they watched through fieldglasses and noted that some of the animals were in their prime. This report is interesting because it implied that the dromedaries in southern Arizona were reproducing in a wild state. Camels have been domesticated for several thousand years, their destiny so entwined with that of the humans they serve that nowhere are they known to live in a state of nature. Therefore the animals turned loose in the American West could have been expected to frighten horses and mules, even to attack a person occasionally if in a revengeful mood, only for a maximum period of forty years or so, for such is the lifespan of a dromedary. But the report of the boundary commission of 1901 indicated that the wild camels of the Southwest were reproducing.

And legends have persisted about sightings. In 1913 the crew of a Santa Fe Railroad train swore they had seen a camel near Wickenburg, Arizona. Sixteen years later came a report of a camel stampeding horses near Banning, California (twenty-five miles west of Palm Springs at the base of the Sierra Nevadas). A traveler journeying south from Ajo (in southwestern Arizona) reported that he came upon one lone camel near a water hole, this in the year 1931. So prevalent was the rumor of camels in the

An Indian camp near Fort Yuma, California, where the camels were turned loose. *Courtesy U.S. Signal Corps, National Archives.*

desert country that when the crew of a Hollywood company filming the movie "Blood and Sand" decided one evening after work to take a moonlight ride on the camels being used in the picture, they terrified residents in the vicinity who thought that ghosts were moving about or else that descendants of the Army's dromedary corps were visiting the area. As late as 1941 newspapers carried a story about the sighting of a camel on the east side of the Salton Sea (in southeastern California).[2]

To the present day in Arizona and the desert portion of southern California, there are local citizens who will swear that camels still live in remote areas of the region. Occasionally someone will report seeing the animals personally, whereupon less-believing city dwellers shake their heads and mumble something about rotgut whiskey or the dire effects of too much sunshine. Yet somehow the legend persists whether or not it has any basis in fact.

9
THE CAMEL EXPERIMENT IN RETROSPECT

Prior to 1846 only a handful of Americans had been confronted by desert country. The line of settlement at that time was from Minnesota down through Iowa to Missouri, Arkansas, and East Texas. Not quite 400 enthusiastic pilgrims had made their way to California prior to 1846, and most of them had made the journey by sea; about 4000 were in Oregon after making the long trek by wagon train from Missouri to the Pacific Northwest, and for almost all of them it had been a one-time journey; and a few hundred men, perhaps a thousand, had made the trip to Santa Fe and back as traders. For all other Americans the land they knew was timbered and well watered, and the animals they had were sufficient for ordinary needs. In addition, railroads were no longer a great curiosity as tracks were being laid between the major industrial cities, and rivers carrying steamboats carrying freight and passengers laid open most parts of the nation.

Then came the Mexican War and with it the annexation of the Southwest. This was followed in rapid order by the discovery of gold in California, awakening tens of thousands of people to thoughts of opportunity in the golden West. In crossing the 2000 miles between the Mississippi Valley and the Pacific Coast, these Forty-Niners were forced into an awareness of the geography of the area, but most had no thoughts of repeated crossings. Only the soldiers sent into the desert country to protect these pilgrims from themselves and from Indians had reason to cross the desert again and again. Thus to the Army fell the necessity of experimenting with alternate means of transportation in a region where horses, pack mules, and oxen suffered from great distance and paucity of water.

Historians and intellectuals in the United States traditionally have used the phrase "the military mind" to imply that Army thinking has been rigid, unimaginative, a slave to the past. Yet within a remarkably short time following the acquisition of the West, some officers in the United States Army were showing a remarkable willingness to adapt to the realities of geography in the West; they were advocating the importation of the camel, an animal alien to their own tradition and to that of Western Europe. The harder task was convincing the people's representatives in Congress, but by March 3, 1855, this had been accomplished. Little more than a year later the first shipload of dromedaries had arrived.

And the camels came on a wave of enthusiasm, at least on the part of some people. Newspaper and magazine editors outdid themselves in printing the most fulsome praise of this "ship of the desert." *National Magazine, Hunt's Merchant's Magazine and Commercial Review*, the San Francisco *Daily Alta California*, and others contained stories in the mid 1850s describing the camel as an even better friend to man than the dog or the horse.[1] J. W. Palmer waxed almost lyrical in his article in *Harper's New Monthly Magazine* for October of 1857, writing:

> . . . It is the one-humped, or Arabian, camel that we have in our mind's eye when we read of the Prophet's milk-white darling—of the camel squadrons of Semiramis, and Xerxes's simoom of hedjins—of the proud Mahri stallion, exulting in his pure lineage—of the wind-challenging Nomanieh, the never-failing Bcharieh, the wondrous Ababdeh hedjin, such as he that went from Cairo to

Mecca, nine hundred miles, in nine days, nor paused to eat or drink—of the wrestling Pehlevans, the fierce fighting camels of Neapul and Oude, the artillery-dromedary of the Persian Zembourek, "the wasp"—of the consecrated dish of camel's flesh, privileged to be the repast of the Prophet—of the "cream of camels," poured out in libations to the gods of old Arabia—of camel's milk, fed to the pampered stallions of Haroun-al-Raschid—of camel's blood, dearer than a slave's, drawn to save famishing Bedouins in mid-desert—of fine camel's hair, prized for the shawl-weaving looms of the Shah—of the caravan camel, the merchant-ship of the Sahara, first in the song when the night-bound drivers sing of sand—of the true war-ship of the desert, the courser-dromedary of the fierce Mahratta's rushing razzias.[2]

Yet magazine and newpaper editors and writers, then and now willing to wax enthusiastic over almost any new idea, did not have to work with the animals in the field—or make command decisions which might have given the camel a fair trial.

The Army officers who were convinced that the dromedary would answer all problems of supply and communication in the Southwest were two majors, George Crosman and Henry Wayne. When they approached their superior, Quartermaster General Thomas Jesup, they were rebuffed. Therefore they turned to political lobbying to accomplish their objective, and Senator Jefferson Davis of Mississippi was converted. In 1855, after Davis became secretary of war, he was able to convince Congress to vote money for the attempt, but Commanding General Winfield Scott, Quartermaster General Jesup, and Brevet Major General David E. Twiggs, commanding the Department of Texas, were not convinced nor had they been consulted.

There was even a philosophical difference between Secretary of War Davis and Major Henry C. Wayne. Davis, sitting in Washington, saw the camels as potential "gunships of the desert" on the model of the Persian army; he thought the camel might carry mounted infantry and even serve as a mobile base for small howitzers. His concept of experimenting with the camel "for military purposes" was that the dromedary would become a super-horse; at its best this would create a cavalry capable of ridding the West of Indians, and at least a beast of burden capable of supplying the most remote outpost swiftly and inexpensively.

Wayne, who had actual charge of the animals in Texas when they first were imported, saw the Army's chore to be one of importing, acclimatizing, and breeding the animals, using them only to the extent of dramatizing their worth. Then civilians would be convinced, importing camels in large numbers until they became common servants of Americans. Wayne was a Quartermaster officer, not a line officer concerned with fighting Indians, and he never viewed the animal as a potential weapon.

In any clash between the secretary of war and a major of Quartermaster, the view that prevails under the Constitution of the United States is that of the cabinet officer in Washington. Wayne's connection with the project ended in January of 1857; thereafter the camels were assigned an active role in transporting supplies for surveyors of wagon roads and for topographical engineers engaged in survey operations, in carrying dispatches between remote outposts, and in transporting various types of goods to and from Army camps.

Nor had the original enthusiasts of importing camels anticipated how other animals in the United States would react to the smell and sight of these animals from the Middle East. Horses and mules stampeded in terror, throwing riders and wrecking wagons. Soon teamsters throughout the West developed an enduring hatred for the dromedary—as did the Army packers assigned·to work with them in a direct way. Because of the camel's hump, it had to be packed different from a mule, and few—if any—enlisted men of that era had experience with distributing freight around a hump and a saddle with a large hole in the center. Nor were these men likely to develop a fast friendship with an animal so prone to spit without provocation, so odorous, and so capable of defending itself from an occasional kick when a packer's temper flared.

In truth, the soldiers and teamsters of the West, those assigned to work with the camel on a one-to-one basis, were horse-minded. These men came from a culture which held that a horse was a noble animal, one which a gentleman rode; this concept dated from the days of chivalry and knighthood, and was not to be changed overnight. They would tolerate a mule, but a horse they could respect, even love. They could talk for hours about the relative merits of one horse over another, discussing withers and fetlocks and gaits. Major Wayne might argue that they only needed a proper introduction to the camel to become friends and admirers of it, but he was arguing against 2000 years of history and tradition.

Neither was Wayne ever able to convince the generals who might have imposed the camel on the troops. David E. Twiggs, sitting in his office in San Antonio, was most eager to get the dromedaries at Camp Verde out of his command, writing time and again that a mule was superior as a packing animal and a horse much better for riding. Quartermaster General Jesup in Washington knew that the secretary of war wanted the animals given a fair trial, and he acquiesced to the inevitable, never fighting the idea openly but also never giving any encouragement to it. And Commanding General Winfield Scott gave nothing, only an imperial silence on the entire subject.

Another source of potential help for the project likewise was not forthcoming. Civilians who might have had influence seemed only interested in making money, writing time and again to indicate a willingness to import the animals for the government at exorbitant fees. Those businessmen who did bring animals, such as Otto Esche of San Francisco, did so more to turn a fast profit rather than to give the camel a fair trial.

Despite these difficulties, the camels that were imported performed admirably. Those officers assigned to work with them in the field were unstinting in their praise. Beale called the camel "an economical and noble brute," while Lieutenant Edward L. Hartz commented, "The patience, endurance, and steadiness which characterize the performance of the camels during the march is beyond praise." In every test the animals showed they could withstand the heat and aridity of the Southwest, perform equally well in mountains and desert, cross mud and rocks, carry great weights, and subsist on plants other animals refused to eat. He was patient in adversity, gentle with children who occasionally were given rides, and obedient so long as well treated; without prodding or beating he would carry from 400 to 600 pounds twenty-five to thirty miles a day, venting his complaint with loud groans only when loaded in the morning. Never did he show physical inability to cope with any aspect of the West—save for the people who mistreated him.

The camel never was widely accepted and used in the American West because he was not native to the area and would have had to be imported in large numbers, and because technology caught up with him too fast. When the Southwest became American in 1848, millions of horses and mules were available for use by pioneers who had a long familiarity with them; camels were a

The camel monument honoring Edward Fitzgerald Beale at Kingman, Arizona. *Courtesy Mohave Pioneer Historical Society.*

curiosity. And the timespan during which the camel might have demonstrated its superiority was too short, less than forty years. The first transcontinental railroad was completed in 1869, just twenty-one years after the Southwest was annexed, and by 1885 the Southern Pacific, Santa Fe, and Northern Pacific had been completed from the Mississippi Valley to the Pacific. Neither horse nor camel could compete with this invention of a technological civilization. Mules and oxen would gradually disappear as machinery came to serve man for transportation and agricultural power; the horse would endure more as a pet and racing animal than as a work animal. Camels never had a chance to demonstrate their capacities in any of these areas. That they were used even so briefly in a limited way is a tribute to the flexibility of mind of some Army officers and politicians.

The camel experiment did generate one curious sidelight. On February 14, 1861, King Mongkut of Siam (later to be romanticized in a stage play and movie entitled "The King and I") wrote to President James Buchanan:

. . . Though formerly there were no Camels on the continent the Americans have sought for and purchased them, some from Arabia, some from Europe, and now camels propagate their race and are serviceable and of benefit to the Country, and are already numerous in America.

Having heard this it has occurred to us that, if on the continent of America there should be several pairs of young male and female elephants turned loose in forests where there was an abundance of water and grass in any region under the Sun's declination both North and South, called by the English the Torrid Zone, . . . we are of the opinion that after a while they will increase till there be large herds. . . .

By the time this letter arrived in Washington, President Buchanan had ended his term of office and replaced by Abraham Lincoln. Despite the fact that the Civil War then was raging with severe Union losses, Lincoln paused from his duties to answer. On February 3, 1862, he replied, "Our political jurisdiction . . .

does not reach a latitude so low as to favor the multiplication of the elephant, and steam on land, as well as on water, has been our best and most efficient agent of transportation in internal commerce." [3]

Steam harnessed by railroad and boat indeed would prove superior to any form of animal power, even that of the elephant, and would open the United States to rapid settlement and development. However, for the urbanized and industrialized citizen of the modern era, it is romantic—and even comforting—to think that in remote areas of the desert Southwest there may be wild camels, descendants of those who originally wore the Army's "U.S." brand.

NOTES

Chapter I

1   For details of these explorations, see Donald Jackson (ed.), *Journals of Zebulon Montgomery Pike with Letters and Related Documents* (Norman: University of Oklahoma Press, 1966); and Edwin James, *An Account from Pittsburgh to the Rocky Mountains* (3 vols., Philadelphia, 1823).

2   Cave J. Couts, *From San Diego to the Colorado in 1849: the Journal and Maps of Cave J. Couts*, ed. by William McPherson (Los Angeles: The Zamorano Club, 1932), 48–49.

3   Josiah Gregg, *Commerce on the Prairies*, ed. by Max Moorhead (Norman: University of Oklahoma Press, 1954), 127.

4   Quoted in Ralph P. Bieber, *Southern Trails to California in 1849* (Glendale, Cal.: Arthur Clark Company, 1937), 306–7.

5   Captain Rufus Ingalls to Major General Thomas Jesup, Denmark, Maine, September 9, 1853, in Fort Yuma Correspondence, National Archives, RG 94 (microfilm copy). Other estimates of the costs involved in moving goods to Fort Yuma were slightly lower.

6   *Congressional Globe*, XXV (1855–56), 1297–99.

7   E. F. Miller to Captain George H. Crosman, Ipswich, Massachusetts, April

24, 1843, Camel File, Old Army and Navy Records Branch, National Archives. A copy is in Albert H. Greenly, "Camels in America," *The Papers of the Bibliographical Society of America*, XLVI, 355–56.

8 This correspondence is in the Camel File, Old Army and Navy Records Branch, National Archives. Hereafter cited as Camel File, OANRB.

9 Charles F. Lummis, *The Land of Poco Tiempo* (New York, 1893), 198.

10 George P. Marsh, *The Camel: His Organization, Habits and Uses, Considered with Reference to His Introduction into the United States* (Boston: Gould and Lincoln, 1856), 30–63.

11 *Ibid.*, 64–66.

12 See Colonel F. Colombari, "The Zemboureks, or the Dromedary Field Artillery of the Persian Army," *Senate Executive Document 62* (Part III), 34 Cong., 3 Sess., 201–38.

13 Marsh, *The Camel*, 122.

Chapter II

1 William H. Powell, *List of Officers of the Army of the United States from 1779 to 1900* (New York, 1900), 265.

2 *Ibid.*, 659.

3 Carl Schurz, *The Reminiscences of Carl Schurz* (3 vols., New York, 1908), II, 21.

4 For details of his life, See Hudson Strode, *Jefferson Davis* (3 vols., New York, 1955–64).

5 John Russell Bartlett, *Personal Narrative of Exploration and Incidents . . .* (2 vols., New York, 1854), II, 576–77.

6 Henry C. Wayne to Jefferson Davis, Washington, November 21, 1853, Camel File, OANRB; also quoted in Dunbar Rowland (ed.), *Jefferson Davis, Constitutionalist: His Letters, Papers and Speeches* (10 vols., Jackson, Miss.: Mississippi Department of Archives and History, 1923), II, 288–90.

7 Jefferson Davis, "Report of the Secretary of War," December 1, 1853, *House Executive Document 1* (Part II), 33 Cong., 1 Sess., 25.

8 Gwinn Harris Heap, *Central Route to the Pacific, from the Valley of the Mississippi to California: Journal of the Expedition of E. F. Beale, Supt. Indian Affairs in California, and Gwinn Harris Heap, from Missouri to California, in 1853* (Philadelphia, 1854), 128–31.

9 Bartlett, *Personal Narrative*, II, 576–84.

10 See March, *The Camel*.

11 Joseph Warren Fabens, *The Camel Hunt: A Narrative of Personal Adventure*

(New York, 1853; new edition). In 1865 Fabens published *The Uses of the Camel; Considered with a View to His Introduction in Our Western States and Territories* (New York, 1865).

12 W. G. Snethen to Davis, series of letters, August 4 to October 5, 1853, Camel File, OANRB.

13 A copy is in Camel File, OANRB.

14 American Camel Company, *Charter of the American Camel Company, Granted by the State of New York; with the Natural History of the Camel* (New York: Published by the Company, 1854), Camel File, OANRB. See also Charles C. Carroll, *The Government's Importation of Camels: A Historic Sketch* (Washington: Department of Agriculture, Bureau of Animal Industry Circular No. 53, 1904), 393.

15 Davis, "Report of the Secretary of War," December 1, 1854, *House Executive Document 1* (Part II), 33 Cong., 2 Sess., 8.

16 *Congressional Globe*, XXX (33 Cong., 2 Sess.), 138.

17 *Ibid.*, 380.

18 *Ibid.*, 1020.

19 A copy of this act is in Appendix, *Congressional Globe*, XXXI (33 Cong., 2 Sess.), 398–99.

20 Until 1947, when the Department of Defense was organized, the secretary of war and the secretary of the navy each had cabinet rank.

21 Letter from Bureau of Supplies and Accounts, Office of Naval Records and Library, Navy Department.

22 For details of Beale's life, see Stephen Bonsal, *Edward Fitzgerald Beale: A Pioneer in the Path of Empire, 1822–1903* (New York, 1912).

23 See Dumas Malone (ed.), *Dictionary of American Biography* (20 vols., New York, 1928–36), XV, 85–88.

24 Davis to Wayne, Washington, May 10, 1855, Camel File, OANRB. Some of the correspondence that follows was printed in *Senate Executive Document 62*, 34 Cong., 3 Sess.

25 This was the Crimean War.

26 Davis to Porter, Washington, May 16, 1855, Camel File, OANRB.

27 Wayne to Davis, New York, May 18, 1855, Camel File, OANRB.

28 Cris Emmett, *Texas Camel Tales* (Austin, Texas: Steck-Vaughn, 1969), 10.

29 Wayne to Davis, London, June 7, 1855, and Paris, July 4, 1855, Camel File, OANRB.

30 Emmett, *Texas Camel Tales*, 10–11.

31 Wayne to Davis, At Sea, July 27, 1855, Camel File, OANRB.

32 J. C. Dobbin to Porter, Washington, May 23, 1855, Camel File, OANRB.

33   Wayne to Davis, Off the Goletta, Gulf of Tunis, August 10, 1855, Camel File, OANRB.

34   Greenly, "Camels in America," 330–31; see also Robert J. Minnon to Davis, Treasury Department, July 12, 1856, Camel File, OANRB.

Chapter III

1   Wayne to Davis, Off the Goletta, Gulf of Tunis, August 10, 1855, Camel File, OANRB.

2   Porter to Davis, Malta, August 13, 1855; and Wayne to Davis, Constantinople, October 3, 1855, Camel File, OANRB.

3   Wayne to Davis, Constantinople, October 31, 1855, Camel File, OANRB.

4   See various letters for time indicated, Camel File, OANRB.

5   Wayne to Davis, Smyrna, January 31, 1856, Camel File, OANRB.

6   Heap to Wayne, Alexandria, December 27, 1855, Camel File, OANRB; also quoted in Greenly, "Camels in America," 358.

7   March, *The Camel*, 68–69.

8   *Ibid.*, 39.

9   Wayne to Davis, Smyrna, January 31, 1856, Camel File, OANRB.

10   *Ibid.*

11   Wayne to Davis, Smyrna, February 8, 1856, Camel File, OANRB.

12   Wayne to Davis, Smyrna, February 11, 1856, Camel File, OANRB.

13   Wayne to Davis, Smyrna, February 8, 1856, Camel File, OANRB.

14   Wayne to Davis, At Sea, May 5, 1856, Camel File, OANRB.

15   Porter to Davis, New York, May 28, 1856, Camel File, OANRB.

16   Wayne to Davis, At Sea, April 10, 1856, Camel File, OANRB.

17   Greenly, "Camels in America," 334–35.

18   Wayne to Davis, Powder Horn, May 1, 1856, Camel File, OANRB.

19   Wayne to Davis, At Sea, May 5, 1856, Camel File, OANRB.

20   *Ibid.*, and Wayne to Davis, Indianola, Texas, May 14, 1856, Camel File, OANRB; see also "Daily Journal Kept on the Camel Deck of the United States Ship Supply," *Senate Executive Document 62*, 34 Cong., 3 Sess., 141.

21   Wayne to General George T. Jesup, Indianola, May 17, 1856; and Wayne to Davis, Indianola, May 17, 1856, Camel File, OANRB.

22   Porter to Davis, New York, May 28, 1856, Camel File, OANRB.

23   Davis to De Leon, Washington, June 18, 1856, Camel File, OANRB.

24 Davis to Porter, Washington, June 26, 1856; and Jesup to Porter, Washington, July 14, 1856, Camel File, OANRB.

25 De Leon to Davis, Alexandria, August 14, 1856, Camel File, OANRB.

26 Porter to Davis, United States Ship "Supply," September 11, 1856, Camel File, OANRB.

27 Greenly, "Camels in America," 338–39.

28 A copy of this contract, signed by Porter and witnessed by Heap, is in Camel File, OANRB.

29 Porter to Davis, Smyrna, November 14, 1856, Camel File, OANRB.

30 Porter to Davis, Malta, December 3, 1856, Camel File, OANRB.

31 Porter to Davis, Mouth of the Mississippi, January 30, 1857, Camel File, OANRB.

32 W. K. Van Bokkelen to Davis, Indianola, February 10, 1857, Camel File, OANRB.

Chapter IV

1 Quoted in Emmett, *Texas Camel Tales*, 31.

2 Marsh, *The Camel*, 73.

3 Emmett, *Texas Camel Tales*, 30.

4 *Ibid.*, 32.

5 Wayne to Davis, Indianola, June 2, 1856, Camel File, OANRB.

6 Marsh, *The Camel*, 72.

7 Porter to Davis, New York, May 28, 1856, Camel File, OANRB.

8 Wayne to Davis, At Sea, April 10, 1856, Camel File, OANRB, describes this.

9 Wayne to Davis, San Antonio, August 12, 1856, Camel File, OANRB, quotes this letter. Pauline Shirkey's reminiscence of these events is in Emmett, *Texas Camel Tales*, 38–41.

10 Emmett, *Texas Camel Tales*, 41–42.

11 Wayne to Davis, San Antonio, June 19, 1856, Camel File, OANRB.

12 Wayne to Davis, San Antonio, June 28, 1856, Camel File, OANRB.

13 Davis to Wayne, Washington, July 5, 1856, Camel File, OANRB.

14 Wayne to Davis, San Antonio, July 22, 1856, Camel File, OANRB.

15 Wayne to Davis, San Antonio, July 28, 1856, Camel File, OANRB.

16 Wayne to Davis, San Antonio, August 4, 1856, Camel File, OANRB.

17 Powell, *List of Officers of the Army*, 517.

18   Wayne to Davis, San Antonio, August 12, 1856, Camel File, OANRB.

19   Wayne to Davis, Camp Verde, August 30, 1856, Camel File, OANRB.

20   Certified statement of expenses submitted by Wayne for the months noted, Camel File, OANRB.

21   Marsh, *The Camel*, 71.

22   "Notes Upon the Camel, collected from 'Reports Upon the Use of the Camel in Algiers,' by General J. L. Carbuccia of the French Army," in *Senate Executive Document 62*, 34 Cong., 3 Sess., 89.

23   Wayne to Davis, Camp Verde, November 5, 1856, Camel File, OANRB.

24   Wayne to Davis, Camp Verde, November 20, 1856, Camel File, OANRB.

25   Wayne to Davis, Camp Verde, December 4, 1856, Camel File, OANRB.

26   Davis to Wayne, Washington, December 13, 1856, Camel File, OANRB.

27   Wayne to Davis, Indianola, January 4, 1857; Wayne to Davis, Washington, February 21, 1857; and Wayne to Quartermaster General Jesup, Washington, February 12, 1857, Camel File, OANRB.

28   Joseph R. Smith to Wayne, Camp Verde, January 29, 1857; and Palmer to Wayne, Camp Verde, January 30, 1857, Camel File, OANRB.

Chapter V

1   Malone (ed.), *Dictionary of American Biography*, VI, 482–83.

2   *Congressional Globe*, XXVI (1856–57), 611–12; see also *U. S. Statutes at Large*, XI, 162.

3   "Correspondence relating to the case of Edward F. Beale," *Senate Executive Document 69*, 34 Cong., 3 Sess., 6.

4   May Humphreys Stacey's journal is contained in Lewis Burt Lesley, *Uncle Sam's Camels: The Journal of May Humphreys Stacey, Supplemented by the Report of Edward Fitzgerald Beale, 1857–1858* (Cambridge: Harvard University Press, 1929), 34. Unless otherwise noted, the incidents in this chapter are from this diary.

5   Major D. H. Vinton to Thomas S. Jesup, San Antonio, February 13, 1857, Camel File, OANRB.

6   Van Bokkelen to Vinton, Indianola, March 5, 1857, Camel File, OANRB.

7   Clay to Vinton, Indianola, April 24, 1857, Camel File, OANRB.

8   Beale, "Wagon Road from Fort Defiance to the Colorado River," *House Executive Document 124*, 35 Cong., 1 Sess., 15.

9   Beale to Floyd, San Elizario, Texas, July 24, 1857, Camel File, OANRB.

10   Beale to Floyd, Colorado River, October 19, 1857, Camel File, OANRB.

11   Beale to Floyd, Colorado River, October 18, 1857, Camel File, OANRB.

12   Johnson deserves far more recognition than he has received for his role in opening the Colorado to steam navigation. See his autobiographical sketch and the Johnson File, both in the Arizona Historical Society, Tucson.

13   Beale's report was printed as *House Executive Document 124*, 35 Cong., 1 Sess., and also is available in Lesley, *Uncle Sam's Camels*, 139–281.

14   Wayne to Jesup, Philadelphia, December 10, 1857, Camel File, OANRB.

15   Palmer to Floyd, Camp Verde, July 31, 1857, Camel File, OANRB.

16   Powell, *List of Officers of the Army*, 640; see also Walter Prescott Webb (ed.), *Handbook of Texas* (2 vols., Austin: Texas State Historical Association, 1952), II, 812.

17   Vinton to Chambliss, San Antonio, August 28, 1857; Chambliss to Vinton, Camp Verde, September 10, 1857; and Twiggs to Assistant Adjutant General, San Antonio, October 10, 1857, in Camel File, OANRB.

18   Twiggs to Jesup, San Antonio, January 13, 1858, Camel File, OANRB.

19   Palmer to Jesup, Camp Verde, October 15, 1857, Camel File, OANRB.

20   Palmer to Floyd, Camp Verde, May 3, 1858, Camel File, OANRB.

21   Vinton to Jesup, San Antonio, June 26, 1858, Camel File, OANRB.

22   Vinton to Jesup, San Antonio, July 8, 1858, Camel File, OANRB.

23   Floyd, "Report of the Secretary of War," Washington, December 5, 1857, *House Executive Document 2*, 35 Cong., 1 Sess., 14.

24   Floyd, "Report of the Secretary of War," Washington, December 6, 1858, *House Executive Document 2*, 35 Cong., 2 Sess., 14; and *Senate Executive Document 2*, 35 Cong., 2 Sess., 14. Hakekyan Bey's treatise can be found in both, pp. 454–91.

25   Meade to Floyd, Camp Verde, May 14, 1858, Camel File, OANRB.

26   These letters are in Camel File, OANRB.

27   *Ibid.*

28   Fisher to Floyd, Baltimore, October 24, 1857, Camel File, OANRB.

29   Ewell to Captain C. L. Easton, Santa Fe, October 12, 1857; and Easton to Jesup, Santa Fe, October 13, 1857, Camel File, OANRB.

Chapter VI

1   For details, see Beale, "Wagon Road—Fort Smith to Colorado River," March 8, 1860, *House Executive Document 42*, 36 Cong., 1 Sess., 91pp. See also Greenly, "Camels in America," 345–59.

2   Clarke to Jesup, San Francisco, February 4, 1859, and endorsement by Jesup, Camel File, OANRB.

Notes

3 "Letters in relation to and Estimate for maintaining camels turned over to the Q.M.'s Dept. at Fort Tejon, Cal., November 17, 1859," Camel File, OANRB.

4 Sacramento *Daily Union,* October 10, 1860.

5 *Ibid.,* September 29 and October 15, 1860.

6 Mowry to Floyd, Washington, August 17, 1860, and Floyd's endorsement, Camel File, OANRB.

7 William H. Brewer, *Up and Down California in 1860–1864,* ed. by Francis P. Farquhar (New Haven: Yale University Press, 1930), 41.

8 Hayes Collection, "Southern California, 1860–1863," Vol. VIII, Doc. 159, as cited in A. A. Gray, "Camels in California," *California Historical Society Quarterly,* IX (December 1930), 307.

9 Details are in Gray, "Camels in California," 316–17.

10 Harlan D. Fowler, *Camels to California* (Stanford, Cal.: Stanford University Press, 1950), 74–76.

11 Galveston *Daily Civilian,* January 5, 1859.

12 For details of this curious incident, see Earl W. Fornell, "A Cargo of Camels in Galveston," *Southwestern Historical Quarterly,* LIX (July 1955), 40–45.

13 Twiggs to Jesup, San Antonio, December 22, 1858, Camel File, OANRB.

14 Emmett, *Texas Camel Tales,* 92.

15 *Ibid.,* 86.

16 Francis R. Lubbock, *Six Decades in Texas,* ed. by C. W. Raines (Austin: B. C. Jones & Co., 1900), 238–42; and Webb (ed.), *Handbook of Texas,* I, 275.

17 Emmett, *Texas Camel Tales,* 96–97.

18 *Ibid.,* 95.

19 Twiggs to Jesup, San Antonio, January 31, 1859, Camel File, OANRB.

20 Twiggs to Jesup, San Antonio, March 29, 1859, Camel File, OANRB.

21 Vinton to Jesup, San Antonio, April 11, 1859, Camel File, OANRB.

22 Powell, *List of Officers of the Army,* 360.

23 Vinton to Act. Asst. Quarter Master of the Escort to the Reconnoissance under Lieut. Echols, Topl. Engrs., San Antonio, April 26, 1859, Camel File, OANRB.

24 Vinton to Twiggs, San Antonio, August 23, 1859, Camel File, OANRB, contains a partial report of the expedition; the full report is in Vinton to Twiggs, San Antonio, September 3, 1859, Camel File, OANRB. A printed version filled with some obvious typographical errors is in *House Executive Document 2,* 36 Cong., 1 Sess., 424–41. Echols' version of the expedition is in "Report of the Secretary of War," Washington, December 3, 1860, *Senate Executive Document 1,* 36 Cong., 2 Sess., 34–51.

25 Palmer to Floyd, Camp Verde, May 20, 1857, Camel File, OANRB.

26 Palmer to Tompkins, Camp Verde, July 8, 1857, Camel File, OANRB.

27 Tompkins to Jesup, New Orleans, August 7, 1857, Camel File, OANRB.

28 Based on a series of letters in Camel File, OANRB.

29 F. Ekerlin to Heap, Chester, Pa., November 17, 1859; Heap to Sibley, Washington, December 3, 1859; and Jesup to Davidson, Washington, January 17, 1860, Camel File, OANRB.

30 Vinton to Quarter Master General J. E. Johnston, San Antonio, October 30, 1860, Camel File, OANRB.

31 John B. Floyd, "Report of the Secretary of War," Washington, December 1, 1859, *Senate Executive Document 2*, 36 Cong., 1 Sess., 6.

Chapter VII

1 Twiggs to Lieut. Col. L. Thomas, San Antonio, December 20, 1860, Camel File, OANRB.

2 Gaylee to Schofield, Headquarters, Department of Missouri, June 15, 1863; and Schofield, memorandum endorsement, July 1, 1863, Camel File, OANRB.

3 Ramsey to Genrl. Granger, San Antonio, July 19, 1865, Camel File, OANRB.

4 Letters and telegrams, July 19, 1865, to March 9, 1866, Camel File, OANRB.

5 Webb, *Handbook of Texas*, I, 409.

6 For details of Coopwood's use of the camels, see Emmett, *Texas Camel Tales*, 153–200.

7 Stockton to Commanding Officer at Camp Latham, Los Angeles, August 25, 1862, Camel File, OANRB.

8 Babbitt to Drum, San Francisco, November 7, 1862, Camel File, OANRB.

9 Maurice H. and Marco R. Newmark (eds.), *Sixty Years in Southern California, 1853–1913, Containing the Reminiscences of Harris Newmark* (revised edition, New York, 1926), 316–17.

10 Bennett to Drum, Camp Drum, May 21, 1863; and Lt. D. J. Williamson to Babbitt, Fort Mojave, June 23, 1862, Camel File, OANRB. See also *The War of the Rebellion: A Compilation of the Official Records of the Union and Confederate Armies* (128 vols., Washington, 1880–1901), Series I, L (Part II), 451–52.

11 Babbitt to Meigs, San Francisco, August 7, 1863, Camel File, OANRB.

12 Morris to Babbitt, Wilmington, California, November 19, 1863, Camel File, OANRB.

13 Babbitt to Meigs, San Francisco, February 27, 1864, Camel File, OANRB.

14 This name also was spelled McLeneghan in many contemporary accounts; I have used the name as it appeared in the documents in Camel File, OANRB.

15 Harlan D. Fowler, *Camels to California: A Chapter in Western Transportation* (Stanford, Cal.: Stanford University Press, 1950), 73.

16 Sacramento *Daily Union*, April 2, 4, 8, 1864.

17 Quoted in Carroll, *The Government's Importation of Camels*, 407.

18 Bonsal, *Edward Fitzgerald Beale*, 207.

19 This quote from the *Daily Territorial Enterprise* of July 6, 1876, is in Gray, "Camels to California," 312.

20 Reno *Nevada State Journal*, June 10, 1909; and Gray, "Camels to California," 313.

21 Lesley, *Uncle Sam's Camels*, 134, states that the Frenchman ranching in Nevada "rounded up between twenty and thirty of the animals near Tucson, Arizona, broke then to pack, and took them to Virginia City, Nevada." Sharlot M. Hall, "Camels in Arizona," *Land of Sunshine*, VIII (February 1898), makes a similar statement.

22 Fowler, *Camels in California*, states that this was Tuili, but such is doubtful.

23 Dan DeQuille, "Camels in the Mines," *New Mexico Historical Review*, XXIV (January 1949), 58–61.

24 *Ibid.*, 55–58.

25 Gray, "Camels in California," 315.

26 Charles F. Lummis, "Pioneer Transportation in America," *McClure's Magazine*, XXVI (November 1905), 90–92. See also Fowler, *Camels to California*, 79.

27 Hadji Ali to Schofield, Camp McDowell, July 3, 1870, and endorsement, Camel File, OANRB.

28 Velma Rudd Hoffman, "Lt. Beale and the Camel Caravans Through Arizona," *Arizona Highways*, XXXIII (October 1957), 12; and Samuel Siciliano, "The Coming of the Camels," *Arizona Highways*, XXXII (May 1956), 32–33.

29 Fowler, *Camels to California*, 88, quotes an article by J. Marvin Hunter in the *Frontier Times* of 1941 to this effect.

30 Gray, "Camels in California," 312.

Chapter VIII

1 Kingman, Arizona, *Mohave County Miner*, February 25, 1893. See also Robert Froman, "The Red Ghost," *American Heritage*, XII (April 1961), 35–37, 94–98.

2 Various newspaper clippings in Camel File, OANRB. See also C. C. Smith, "Camels in the Southwest," *Arizona Historical Review*, I (1929), 90–96.

Chapter IX

1   See G. P. Disosway, *National Magazine*, XI (December 1857), 481–88; W. G. King, "Commercial Value of the Camel," *Hunt's Merchants Magazine and Commercial Review*, XXX (June 1854), 659–60; and San Francisco *Daily Alta California*, December 30, 1856, January 4, February 14, and March 29, 1857.

2   J. W. Palmer, "The Ship of the Desert," *Harper's New Monthly Magazine*, XV (October 1857), 582.

3   A. B. Moffatt, *King Mongkut of Siam* (Ithaca, N.Y.: Cornell University Press, 1961), 92–95.

BIBLIOGRAPHY

The major source for the story of the Army's experiment with camels, from importation to final auction, is the Camel File of the Old Army and Navy Records Branch of the National Archives, supplemented by reports printed in government documents. The bibliography that follows includes only those items I found particularly helpful; it does not reflect all the materials I examined. In my reading of the many secondary accounts of the camel experiment on the Southwestern frontier, I often was reminded of the mythical Chinese kingdom where the citizens made their living by taking in each other's laundry; most of the articles in popular journals—and some in scholarly ones—have repeated the same few stories readily available in government documents. I have not included most of them in the bibliography that follows. Those interested in pursuing these ephemeral articles and books should consult the bibliographies in the following two sources:

Greenly, Albert H. "Camels in America," *The Papers of the Bibliographical Society of America*, XLVI (1952), 327–72. The bibliography is on pp. 359–72.

Lewis, William S. "A Contribution Towards a Bibliography of the Camel, With Particular Reference to the Introduction of Camels into the United States and the Camel Pack Trains in the Western Mining Camps," *California Historical Society Quarterly*, IX (December 1930), 336–44.

Manuscript Sources

Beale, Edward Fitzgerald. Biographical File. Arizona Historical Society, Tucson.

Camel File. Old Army and Navy Records Branch, National Archives. This contains more than a thousand manuscript pages, including letters pertaining to camels prior to congressional approval of the experiment in 1855, reports and letters from the field, and even newspaper clippings about alleged sightings of wild camels in the twentieth century.

Johnson, George A. Autobiographical sketch. Arizona Historical Society, Tucson.

————. Biographical File. Arizona Historical Society, Tucson.

Ingals, Rufus. Letter to Major General Thomas Jesup, Denmark, Maine, September 9, 1853. Fort Yuma Correspondence, National Archives, RG 94. Microfilm copy.

Tedro, Philip (Hi Jolly). Biographical File. Arizona Historical Society, Tucson.

Government Documents

Beale, Edward Fitzgerald. "Wagon Road from Fort Defiance to the Colorado River," *House Executive Document* 124, 35 Cong., 1 Sess. Also available in Lewis Burt Lesley (ed.), *Uncle Sam's Camels: The Journal of May Humphreys Stacey, Supplemented by the Report of Edward Fitzgerald Beale, 1857–1858* (Cambridge, Mass.: Harvard University Press, 1929), 139–281.

————. "Wagon Road—Fort Smith to Colorado River," *House Executive Document 42*, 36 Cong., 1 Sess.

Congressional Globe, XXX (1854–55); XXXI (Appendix, 1854–55); XXXV (1855–56); XXXVI (1856–57).

"Correspondence Relating to the Case of Edward F. Beale," *Senate Executive Document 69*, 34 Cong., 3 Sess.

Davis, Jefferson. "Report of the Secretary of War," December 1, 1853, *House Executive Document 1* (Part II), 33 Cong., 1 Sess.

————. "Report of the Secretary of War," December 1, 1854, *House Executive Document 1* (Part II), 33 Cong., 2 Sess.

Echols, William. Report of his topographical survey of the Big Bend, in *Senate Executive Document 1*, 36 Cong., 2 Sess., 34–51.

Floyd, John B. "Report of the Secretary of War," December 5, 1857, *House Executive Document 2*, 35 Cong., 1 Sess.

————. "Report of the Secretary of War," December 6, 1858, *House Executive Document 2*, 35 Cong., 2 Sess.; and *Senate Executive Document 2*, 35 Cong., 2 Sess.

Bibliography

Floyd, John B. "Report of the Secretary of War," December 1, 1859, *Senate Executive Document 2*, 36 Cong., 1 Sess.

Hartz, Edward L. Report on the use of camels in surveying the Big Bend, in *House Executive Document 2*, 36 Cong., 1 Sess., 424–41.

Senate Executive Document 62, 34 Cong., 2 Sess. This contains letters and documents relating to the two expeditions to secure camels from the Middle East, along with a few letters from Camp Verde about the early experiments there.

The War of the Rebellion: A Compilation of the Official Records of the Union and Confederate Armies. 128 vols. Washington, 1880–1901.

Printed Original Sources

American Camel Company. *Charter of the American Camel Company, Granted by the State of New York; with the Natural History of the Camel.* New York: Published by the Company, 1854.

Bartlett, John Russell. *Personal Narrative of Exploration and Incidents in Texas, New Mexico, California, Sonora and Chihuahua, 1850–1853.* New York, 1854.

Brewer, William H. *Up and Down California in 1860–1864*, ed. by Francis F. Farquhar. New Haven, Conn.: Yale University Press, 1930.

Couts, Cave J. *From San Diego to the Colorado in 1849: The Journal and Maps of Cave J. Couts*, ed. by William McPherson. Los Angeles: The Zamorano Club, 1932.

Heap, Gwinn Harris. *Central Route to the Pacific, from the Valley of the Mississippi to California: Journal of the Expedition of E. F. Beale, Supt. Indian Affairs in California, and Gwinn Harris Heap, from Missouri to California in 1853.* Philadelphia, 1854.

Jackson, Donald (ed.). *Journals of Zebulon Montgomery Pike with Letters and Related Documents.* Norman: University of Oklahoma Press, 1966.

James, Edwin. *An Account from Pittsburgh to the Rocky Mountains.* 3 vols. Philadelphia, 1823.

Lubbock, Francis R. *Six Decades in Texas*, ed. by C. W. Raines. Austin, Tex.: B. C. Jones & Co., 1900.

Newmark, Maurice H., and Marco R. *Sixty Years in Southern California, 1853–1913, Containing the Reminiscences of Harris Newmark.* New York, 1926, revised edition.

Rowland, Dunbar (ed.). *Jefferson Davis, Constitutionalist: His Letters, Papers and Speeches.* 10 vols. Jackson: Mississippi Department of Archives and History, 1923.

Schurz, Carl. *The Reminiscences of Carl Schurz.* 3 vols. New York, 1907–1908.

Stacey, May Humphreys. *Uncle Sam's Camels: The Journal of May Humphreys Stacey,*

Supplemented by the Report of Edward Fitzgerald Beale, *1857–1858*, ed. by Lewis Burt Lesley. Cambridge, Mass.: Harvard University Press, 1929.

Newspapers

Galveston (Texas) *Daily Civilian*
Kingman (Arizona) Mohave County Miner
Los Angeles Star
Oakland Tribune
Reno *Nevada State Journal*
Sacramento (California) *Daily Union*
San Francisco *Daily Alta California*
San Fancisco *Daily Evening Bulletin*
San Francisco *Herald*

Secondary Sources

Bieber, Ralph P. *Southern Trails to California in 1849.* Glendale, Cal.: Arthur Clark Company, 1937.

Bonsal, Stephen. *Edward Fitzgerald Beale: A Pioneer in the Path of Empire.* New York, 1912.

Carroll, Charles C. *The Government's Importation of Camels: A Historic Sketch.* Washington: Department of Agriculture, Bureau of Animal Industry Circular No. 53, 1904.

Colombari, Colonel F. "The Zemboureks, or the Dromedary Field Artillery of the Persian Army," *Senate Executive Document 62* (Part III), 34 Cong., 3 Sess., 201–38.

DeQuille, Dan. "Camels in the Mines," *New Mexico Historical Review,* XXIV (January 1949), 54–61.

Emmett, Cris. *Texas Camel Tales.* Austin: Steck-Vaughn, 1969; edited version of 1932 original.

Fabens, Joseph Warren. *The Camel Hunt: A Narrative of Personal Adventure.* New York, 1853, new edition. Fiction.

———.*The Uses of the Camel: Considered with a View to His Introduction in Our Western States and Territories.* New York, 1865.

Fornell, Earl W. "A Cargo of Camels in Galveston," *Southwestern Historical Quarterly,* LIX (July 1955), 40–45.

Bibliography

Fowler, Harlan D. *Camels to California*. Stanford, Cal.: Stanford University Press, 1950.

Froman, Robert. "The Red Ghost," *American Heritage*, XII (April 1961), 35–37, 94–98.

Gray, A. A. "Camels in California," *California Historical Society Quarterly*, IX (December 1930), 299–317.

Greenly, Albert H. "Camels in America," *The Papers of the Bibliographical Society of America*, XLVI (1952), 327–72.

Gregg, Josiah. *Commerce on the Prairies*, ed. by Max Moorhead. Norman: University of Oklahoma Press, 1954.

Hall, Sharlot M. "Camels in Arizona," *Land of Sunshine*, VIII (February 1898), 122.

Hoffman, Velma Rudd. "Lt. Beale and the Camel Caravans Through Arizona," *Arizona Highways*, XXXIII (October 1957), 7–13.

King, W. G. "Commercial Value of the Camel," *Hunt's Merchants Magazine and Commercial Review*, XXX (June 1854), 659–60.

Lummis, Charles F. *The Land of Poco Tiempo*. New York, 1893.

———. "Pioneer Transportation in America," *McClure's Magazine*, XXVI (November 1905), 90–92.

Malone, Dumas (ed.). *Dictionary of American Biography*. 20 vols., New York, 1928–36.

Marsh, George P. *The Camel: His Organization, Habits and Uses, Considered with Reference to His Introduction into the United States*. Boston: Gould and Lincoln, 1856.

Moffatt, A. B. *King Mongkut of Siam*. Ithaca, N.Y.: Cornell University Press, 1961.

Palmer, J. W. "The Ship of the Desert," *Harper's New Monthly Magazine*, XV (October 1857), 577–93.

Powell, William H. (comp.). *List of Officers of the Army of the United States from 1779 to 1900*. New York, 1900.

Siciliano, Samuel. "The Coming of the Camels," *Arizona Highways*, XXXII (May 1956), 32–33.

Smith, C. C. "Camels in the Southwest," *Arizona Historical Review*, I (1929), 90–96.

Strode, Hudson. *Jefferson Davis*. 3 vols. New York, 1955–64.

Webb, Walter Prescott (ed.). *The Handbook of Texas*. 2 vols. Austin: Texas State Historical Association, 1952.

Woodward, Arthur, and Helen Griffin, *Fort Tejon: A Nursery of the Army*. Los Angeles: Dawson's Book Shop, 1942.

# INDEX

Big Bend (Texas), camels used to survey, 142-50
Bishop, S. A., uses camels, 129-30, 132, 162
Black Beaver (Delaware Indian), 129
Bouquet, Jules V., 140
Breckenridge, A., Jr., 102
British Columbia (Canada), camels in, 137, 164, 169
Brodhead, J. M., 98
Brooks, Joel H., 98
Brownsville (Texas), 155
Buchanan, James, 43, 68, 90, 94, 97, 189
Buffalo, described, 6

Cairo (Egypt), noted, 123; camel expedition at, 50-51, 52
California, noted, 3, 4, 15, 16, 17, 18, 27, 30, 32, 34, 37, 59, 97, 152, 157, 170, 174, 180, 182, 183; camels used to survey wagon road to, 97-117; camels used in, 129-36; civilians use camels in, 136-37; camel herd sold in, 158-60
Calles, Plutarcho Elías, 174
Camel, pictures of, 21, 29, 47, 49, 51, 52, 53, 54, 56, 58, 63, 64, 72, 78, 84, 89, 93, 100, 104, 111, 121, 131, 135, 147, 161, 163, 165, 167; proposed for use in the Southwest, 18-20, 24, 34; described, 20-23; Congress appropriates money for, 34-35; first expedition to import, 35-60; second expedition to import, 61-68; in Texas, 68-94; used to survey wagon road, 95-117; work in Texas, 117-24; offers by civilians to import, 124-27; philosophy of use by Army, 128-29; Army uses of, 129-36; civilians import, 136-41; at Camp Verde, 141-42; used to survey Big Bend, 142-50; discharge of Arabs working with, 150-53; in Texas during Civil War, 154-56; Texas herd sold, 156-58;

California herd sold, 158-60; used by civilians, 160-75; legends about, 176-82; significance of experiment with, 183-90. *See also* Bactrian Camel *and* Dromedary
Camel Transportation Company, proposed, 33-34
Camp Drum (California), camels at, 158
Camp Fitzgerald (California), camels at, 134
Camp Hudson (Texas), camels at, 144
Camp Latham (California), camels at, 158
Camp McDowell (Arizona), 172
Camp Stockton (Texas), camels at, 150
Camp Verde (Texas), noted, 79, 187; described, 80; headquarters for camels, 80-102, 118-24, 127, 139, 141-43, 152, 155, 156
Canales, Antonio, 82
Caralambo, George, hired, 66; works with camels, 132-33, 134, 150, 152, 162; later life of, 170
Carbuccia, L. L., on military uses of camels, 59, 88
Carleton, J. H., and camel use, 132-33
Carling, Hugh, 164
Carson, Kit, 38, 97, 129
Cazneau, William L., offers to supply camels, 124
Chambliss, W. P., 120
Chandler, W. P., 46
Chester (Pennsylvania), 37, 38, 98, 99, 130
Chisholm, Jesse, 129
Cibolo (Texas), 75
Clarke, Newman S., and camel use, 132
Clay, R. E., 100-101
Cocopah (steamboat), picture of, 116
Colorado River, noted, 11, 13, 79, 97, 133; wagon road surveyed to, 97-98, 108-17; camels at, 129-30
Communication, in the West, 16-17